C000254086

Living in PROVENCE

DANE McDOWELL

Photographs by CHRISTIAN SARRAMON

Preface by MICHEL BIEHN

Flammarion

CONTENTS

An ever-changing view—
the Mediterranean as seen
through the shutters of a
villa on Cap Ferrat
(page 1). A view of
Saint-Paul-de-Vence
from the home of an
English architect (pages
2–3). A farm surrounded
by terraced fields in the
countryside behind
Grasse (pages 4–5).
A stately path leads up
to a manor house in the
Alpine foothills (above).
A farm near Saint-Rémy-
de-Provence (right).

LIVING IN PROVENCE

by Michel Biehn

Long ago, many of the houses in Provence were just like tiny stone cubes, made up of a roof and four walls, a shady arbor with a few honey-sweet bunches of grapes (while some would be eaten, the rest would be saved for the wine press), a bench made from a long flat stone, three hollyhocks, a wooden table, and two rush-bottomed chairs brought out for guests. Inside, there would be a bed for taking naps and a fireplace for grilling. Water was brought in from outside. The owners would go there for the day, either because they had to tend the vineyard, or simply for their own pleasure—to watch the grapes ripen, to gather wild herbs and leeks, or to take a brief rest after a long morning's hike through the fields.

Larger houses were often built around wells, their backs facing the cold wind from the north, their fronts soaking up the sunshine from the south. The wings of a hillside house would embrace an inner courtyard that would be evenly paved with round, polished pebbles like a riverbed, its main entrance flanked by cypresses and shaded by stately fig trees. Beyond the house stood terraced olive groves, and orchards of almond and cherry. The fragrance of thyme and lavender was wafted on the breeze from the wild meadows nearby, along with the tolling of church bells and the clang of the village forge.

Houses on the plains were built in jagged lines to form windbreaks against the cold blast of the mistral wind, like the rows of dark cypress trees separating the fields, or the clumps of slender reeds along the creeks. Standing sentinel in front of these houses would be a pair of tall plane or lotus trees, shedding their leaves in winter to let the warm, slanting sunbeams inside. Here and there, tucked behind the broad ribbon of a high wall, a somber forest of cedars and chestnuts might shelter a paradise of pools and fountains, orange trees in tubs, trimmed boxwood, and carefully manicured gravel paths leading to a vast manor house, its façade

The inviting landscape outside Aix contrasts with the barren, violet-hued mountain peaks above it. In Cézanne country, between Mount Sainte-Victoire and Mount Olympe, this Italian-style manor, protected by a barrier of cypress and plane trees in the middle of a vineyard, was erected at the beginning of the twentieth century.

At Mane in the Alpes-de-Haute-Provence, the Château de Sauvan overlooks a formal French park extending over three terraces (above, top). On a plot of land overlooking the gulf of Saint-Tropez, landscape architect Louis Benech has designed a sophisticated garden full of surprises that combines patches of artichoke and lantana (above, bottom).

softly dusted with golden ocher and pierced by rows of high windows. Lovely ladies dressed in white strolled the terraces, hardly ever leaving their vantage point, resting their elbows on the balustrade as they listened idly to the laughing children, and to the barking dogs as they scuffled happily in the cool garden below.

Cabins and huts built in the vineyards or in little seaside coves, farmhouses (known locally as *mas*, *mazets*, *bastides*, and *bastidons*), dovecotes, and mills were the threads from which dreams were spun in those days, and this is even more the case today.

But today, everything has changed. Most of the houses that once rang with the sounds of daily life and toil have now become elegant vacation retreats for visitors from all parts of the world, and their inflated selling prices often place them beyond the reach of local inhabitants. On the other hand, these new owners—who genuinely love the region of Provence and respect its traditions—often do much more to preserve, restore, and beautify the area's heritage than many of the local officials, who have approved rampant construction of mediocre projects and for whom "beautification" is usually limited to the addition of banal and charmless decorations to the new traffic circles from which roads at the entrance to villages now radiate.

But Provence has been changed before. In the eighteenth century, the establishment in Avignon of a schismatic papacy and its brilliant, refined, sybaritic court led to the development of the silk industry in the south of France to satisfy the courtiers' demand for luxurious materials. This was marked by the spread of silkworm-breeding farms and the cultivation of mulberry trees by the thousand in order to supply the ravenous worms with their diet of leaves, a development that profoundly and permanently altered the Provençal landscape. In much the same way, today's newcomers from throughout the world, and their often opulent installations, have engendered, in our own time, spectacular alterations in the landscape, but also the renewal of numerous skills and crafts.

Artisans in the region are now rediscovering ancestral techniques and skills, and revitalizing the bonds between human hand and soul. Masons are once again mastering stone, blacksmiths are returning to their forges, painters are pulverizing their own pigments to create rich colors. Trees are no longer cut back to the stump every winter—pruners are again learning how to sculpt the living branch. "Faux-rustic" swirled stucco is

*The interior courtyard of
a beguiling Lourmarin
shop, the Côté Bastide,
where strollers are invited
to browse among the
vaulted rooms of a fine
manor house that has
been converted into an
exhibition area for
tableware, bath accessories,
and other household
furnishings (left).
In the village of Ménerbes,
the former residence of the
barons of Carmejane,
which dates from the
Renaissance, proudly
raises its fortifications
above the ramparts and
valley below it (above).*

The shores of the
Mediterranean Sea
continue as they have
done for so long to attract
painters, writers, and
celebrities. From the late
nineteenth century,
international royalty
and certain wealthy
eccentrics have elected to
set up home on the few
acres of land on Cap
Ferrat. Béatrice Ephrussi
de Rothschild chose
the upper slopes for the
construction of an opulent
manor in the Florentine
style, filling it with
treasures acquired
throughout the world.
Seven theme-based
gardens form a backdrop
for this palace-by-the-sea
(left). Half native and
half exotic, the luxuriant
vegetation, in which palm
trees and parasol pines
abound, protects the
privacy of Cap Ferrat's
splendid villas (facing
page, left). At Beaulieu-
sur-Mer, the Villa
Kérylos—former
residence of a millionaire
Hellenist—rises above
the Baie des Fourmis
(facing page, right).

being removed, and walls stripped down to the original stone. Ocher, sand, and lime are being blended into subtle hues for the protection of the façades of houses. Furthermore—over and above the rigorous restoration of cabins and farmhouses—architects, interior designers, and landscape architects are also inventing a contemporary vocabulary for contemporary living.

Now, as ever, the spirit of the times is blowing through the region like the mistral wind, consigning successive fads to the oblivion of the past. Although there remain a few isolated areas where the faded and static hand of time lies heavy, Provence has always been at the crossroads between East and West, between Italy and Spain, between Africa and Paris—a mediator between tradition and fashion. Eternally shifting, yet somehow changeless; absorbing varied influences, feeding on them avidly and greedily, but never losing its own identity.

A host of imported techniques, plants, spices, and styles, a host of customs rooted in the ephemera of passing fashion or in a single historical event are now emblematic of this particular land and civilization. For example: in the twelfth century, when the crusaders landed in Palestine, they were stunned by the abundance and beauty of the orange trees they found there. They brought some cuttings back to France, planting them in Hyères, the home port of the crusader ships. The beautiful new tree soon made a fortune for local growers, who used its blossoms for perfume and its fruit for the table, after which Hyères was fittingly given the name

of "Island of Gold." Orange trees throve in the mild climate along the Mediterranean coast, but elsewhere they had to be protected from the rigors of winter. This led to the invention of the orangery and the development by Anduze potters, several centuries later, of their specialty: the oversize glazed earthenware garden tub. The Anduze orange-tree tub is now a fixture in Provençal gardens.

On another occasion, when the Siamese ambassadors passed through Marseilles in 1684 on their way to the court of Louis XIV, the local population was entranced by the beauty of their striped clothing. This marked the inception of *siamoise*, a striped silk-and-cotton fabric which was used for two centuries in the manufacture of clothing for Provençal peasants, and is still used today for the folk costume of Nice: a red-and-white striped skirt and conical straw hat adorned with embroidered mimosa blossoms.

Beyond historical events, beyond its borrowings from other cultures, and new customs; far beyond folklore, pastis, pétanque, and the local accent; and farther still beyond the hues of ocher cliff and lavender field, the silvery glimmer of olive trees through the mistral, the song of locusts under the pines, and the buzz of grasshoppers in the arid brush, the dry-stone walls and antique façades relentlessly eroded by the wind—and despite the injuries inflicted by the passage of time—the beauty of Provence remains eternal and glorious, and living in Provence today is a privilege and a joy.

GARDENS

VISIONS OF PARADISE

Nothing could be more presumptuous than to reshape the landscape according to one's personal vision; to succumb, in the words of Saint-Simon, "to the superb pleasure of mastering nature." The creation of a garden, no matter how small, involves idealizing the world according to a specific image of earthly "paradise"—which is not a completely innocent word, since it is derived from the Persian *pardès*, meaning "pleasure garden."

The image of paradise has already been imposed on Provence and the Côte d'Azur. This fertile land—where vineyards and olive groves have grown since ancient times, and where the almond tree heralds the arrival of spring a month earlier than elsewhere in France—already provides a foretaste of paradise envied by other regions. The artist Nicolas Poussin, for example, set his painting, *Bergers d'Arcadie (Arcadian Shepherds)*, in the Grasse countryside at the foot of the Baou de Saint-Jeannet. However, the region does have at least one climatic drawback: the drought in summer. Agriculture and horticulture depend on the availability of water, which is a rare and unevenly distributed commodity. So the value and beauty of properties in Provence depend on the presence of springs. Spring water quenches the thirsty eye in pools, burbles in fountains, is hoarded in irrigation basins and canals, and drawn up from the depths of wells. Plantings are organized around this exterior sign of wealth, which is responsible for so many miracles.

The gardens of contemporary landscape architects reflect the lessons of their predecessors. The prevailing spirit harks back to the hedonism of a bygone age, although influences and tastes have evolved, and the primary concern today is the good life rather than pure esthetics. From Saint-Tropez to Saint-Rémy, from Grasse to the Mediterranean coast, today's landscapers tame a sun that shines on alleys of plane trees, borders of iris, and beds of roses. They joyfully indulge in a profusion of arbors, pergolas, and trellises, which afford cool shade to go alongside the water held captive in pools and topiary gardens.

Swimming pools and their settings—because of their link with well-being—are treated as obligatory exercises in style. Sometimes they are integrated into the overall design of the garden, like a stone pool that has

Designed by Jean Mus, the garden at Le Moulin affords a marvelous panoramic view of the countryside behind Grasse (preceding double-page). Patricia Wells's garden at Vaison-le-Romaine is arranged around a sapphire-blue pool set in a frame of greenery (facing page). Two stone baskets filled with symbolic fruits overlook the stone staircase (above).

acquired the patina of age; sometimes they are given a tropical accent, like an oasis in the desert. Either way, swimming pools serve as focal points but never detract from the overall harmony.

Small gardens imitate the spectacular creations of landscapers. They constitute, on a reduced scale, a tiny corner of paradise featuring two essential components: water and shade. "Because space is limited, these smaller gardens are more structured," explains Patricia Wells, ambassador for French gastronomy on both sides of the Atlantic, restaurant critic for the *International Herald Tribune*, and author of numerous books on food. The placement of each tree and plant is analyzed with as much care as a theatrical setting. Every detail is a pure pleasure, from the alley of cypress trees that alters the perspective a little, to the rustic bench, placed as if by chance in front of a stunning view.

It is the availability of water that explains the number and quality of the gardens attached to Provençal farmhouses. Property owners were inspired to create pleasure gardens beside their orchards and vegetable patches, and this accounts for the rich horticultural heritage found around Aix-en-Provence and Marseilles from the seventeenth century onward. The gardens of Ansouis and La Gaude, and those surrounding the Enfant and Bidaine pavilions, are among the finest in Provence.

Because of the Italian influence, gardens in the South of France exhibit controlled fluidity and rigor, and are integrated into their environment with instinctive harmony. Exploiting the local topography, they transform the geometry of the land into a sequence of spaces articulated according to original themes and variations based on terraced fields and alleys of cypress and plane trees. A rival influence came from England. On the Côte d'Azur—and particularly around Menton— landscape gardeners Lord Radcliffe and Miss Campbell (at Val Rahmeh), and William Waterfield (at Le Clos du Peyronnet), invented an exotic decor featuring rare trees and plants. Britishers settling in Provence show a preference for the neo-rural English garden that possesses a visual harmony inspired by impressionist painting.

On the Côte d'Azur, the vogue for exotic gardens is an invitation to tour the world, through visits to the Thuret gardens in Antibes, the Handbury gardens in La Mortola, the Champfleury gardens in Cannes, and many others of the same type perched atop the cliffs. Some of these gardens, such as Les Colombières in Menton and the Villa Domergue in

Patricia Wells lives in an extremely charming old mas that is located above Vaison-la-Romaine. The vegetable garden that borders the property plays a starring role; here she grows twenty-four varieties of tomato, in every shape and in every color (left), for which she invents delectable recipes.

Surrounded by ancient outbuildings—including a bake-oven still in use today—the old farmhouse has benefited from a facelift. Aromatic herbs are carefully tended in the garden (above); they make frequent appearances in the cooking courses conducted by Patricia Wells, and in her recent book, My Kitchen in Provence.

Cannes, are inspired by Mediterranean legends. Man is never excluded from this landscape sculpted by dreams. The Provençal garden is a place of freedom, sensuality, and beauty. Overflowing with fragrances, colors, music, and even caresses—the touch of a breeze or rustling wisteria petals—the gardens of the south flatter the eye less than those of the north. Their irresistible appeal is explained, perhaps, by this hidden sensuality combined with profound humanism. Landscape design today no longer obeys the rule of outward appearances, but is cast in a more sophisticated and more intellectual light. Landscape architects explore innovative concepts through a renewed focus on the plants themselves, and on a respect for the local climate and topography. Setting new goals for themselves, these designers present a world that is carefully organized and structured, but free, thus reinventing paradise in their own image.

A pleasure garden dotted with a few cypress trees surrounds Patricia Wells's house. Well-designed but informal, the garden is rustic in mood, accented with boxwood hedges and a rosemary-lined path. The owner likes to entertain in her garden, where she offers guests wine from her own estate, the famed Clos Chanteduc (right, above).

GARDENS BY LANDSCAPE ARCHITECTS

*T*he Provençal paradise is a human invention. With consummate skill and patience, gardeners and landscape architects have succeeded in taming nature and enhancing its beauty. Respectful of a lifestyle conditioned by wind, shade, sun, and water, today's landscape architects—Louis Benech, Gilles Clément, Alex Dingwall-Main, Alain Faragou, Dominique Lafourcade, Arnaud Maurières, Jean Mus, Éric Ossart, and Michel Sémini—have learned from the lessons of the past. Hedonistic rather than purely esthetic; cosmic, playful, and sometimes esoteric, their designs reflect new cultural sources and newly acquired knowledge. Here is a chance to explore some of these secret gardens off the beaten path.

Blue, gray, white: a romantic palette near Grasse

The old olive mill overlooks a landscape of terraced fields. A flute player under the branches of an olive tree charms the goldfish in a pond. Jean Mus's palette is made up primarily of subtle grays, whites, and blues (preceding page). The cheerful burbling of the fountain greets visitors as soon as they enter the courtyard (above).

The garden at Le Moulin, which has been designed by Jean Mus, is a perfect illustration of this renowned artist's talents. Here, the winner of France's highest award in the field of landscape architecture, the Arbre d'Or, invites visitors to sample the subtle sensuality of a masterfully organized tour.

The former olive-oil mill is now a romantic blue-shuttered farmhouse. It looks down over the terraced hills, which are planted with the olive groves that reign supreme in the region.

Behind its rampart of high stone walls, the entrance to the house gives no inkling of the beauties that lie beyond. Only on the far side of the house does the garden comes into view. Although it is just a few seasons old, the height of the trees and luxuriance of the flower beds and shrubbery are such that one would swear it had existed forever. As the visitor continues to explore, the garden seems to blend so seamlessly with the surrounding landscape that it gives the impression that untamed nature has been left virtually untouched. In fact, however, the garden's design was orchestrated by a master hand and obeys a geometry that is as discreet as it is logical.

Two vertical lines—stone staircases shaded by an arbor of Banks roses—form a contrast to the horizontal layers of terraced fields. The staircases are bordered by olive trees, which jealously share their space with rows of lavender. Hidden by beds of immortelle and rosemary, two surprises await visitors at the first terrace level: on one side stands a mossy pool invaded by papyrus and water lilies; on the other hangs a rudimentary swing that has been attached to an olive branch, which recalls the famous painting by Jean-Honoré Fragonard—a native son of the region—produced two centuries earlier.

Beyond lies the swimming pool, a plain rectangle reflecting the color of sky and hillside: blue. Blue, along with gray and white, is one of Jean Mus's favorite colors. This landscape artist's palette is made up of blue—for lavender, iris, wisteria, rosemary, *Choysia temata*, and African lilies; white—for nightshade, thornless Banks roses, and a ravishing variety of heather from the coast; and, lastly, gray—for olive leaves, santolina, and cineraris groundsel. Stronger than all of them, however, is the symphony of greens that dominates the countryside.

Following the contour of the terrain and melting into a terraced field that has been here since time immemorial, the garden has been designed so that nature keeps its rustic and generous side. A bronze statue in a modest pose watches over the stone pool (left). Accented with olive trees and with trimmed boxwood hedges, a path paved with centuries-old stones runs along the length of the main terrace (above).

A cascade of wisteria adds its blue-tinted veil to this terrace, which is particularly appreciated in springtime, when the sun is not yet too hot (left). A stone shepherd, who might have escaped from an eighteenth-century pastoral painting, awaits his shepherdess in the middle of an alley bordered with rosemary bushes and olive trees (above). Illuminated by wrought-iron lanterns, a stone staircase under an arbor of Banks roses leads to the back of the garden (right, top). Breaking with the straight lines of the terraces, boxwood hedges and cinerary groundsel add a soft, sensual note to the overall setting (right, bottom).

Jean Mus composes his gardens with all the passion of an orchestral conductor, referring to them as his "scores." The tempo in this garden is set by powerful notes of cypress, pine, evergreen oak, and olive. The rhythm is slowed by the pauses and sighs of emerald-green lawns and pools of cool dark water, and is then accelerated again by the downward rush of a staircase. Finally it is concluded "con brio" by a wrought-iron summerhouse—a spot for trysts and secrets.

This musical composition is punctuated with musical phrases that form distinct melodic counterpoints: views are framed by groves of everlasting, shady nooks holding graceful rustic statues, stone shepherds and shepherdesses, and—the most lilting of all, hidden behind cascades of Banks roses—a water garden with a pool set like a gem in its jewel-case lawn. Standing between water rushes and cattails, a little flute-player charms the goldfish in the pool.

"Natural surroundings all have their hidden music," says Mus, "but you have to know how to listen for it." This explains the benches that are dotted here and there throughout the garden. They are resting places where visitors can listen for all the sounds modulating the silence around them—a nightingale's song, a breeze rustling the leaves of a palm tree, a silken flutter of owl's wings. This little night music, which floats on the air and clings to the foliage, is interrupted at the same time every evening by a chorus of tree frogs—a vibrant concert that fills the night air until very late, when the stars come out above the blue hills.

The garden at Le Moulin is like a poem celebrating eternity and eternal change, speaking not as a metaphor but with a succession of slight and ephemeral sensations that reflect earthly happiness.

Clumps of agapantha
and pots of impatiens
enliven the privacy of a
little paved courtyard with
their vivid blooms
(above). Echoing the
pattern of the low dry-
stone wall, architect
Hugues Bosc has
designed a swimming
pool in an antique mood.
Cool water, masses of
flowers, and an olive tree
with knotted trunk and
branches heavy with fruit
are emblematic of the
good life as lived in the
Alpine foothills (right).

Pierre Bergé's Mediterranean gardens

Pierre Bergé entrusted the design of his garden at Saint-Rémy to Michel Sémini, a landscape architect whose headquarters are in Goult. It might easily be assumed that Bergé—connoisseur of the arts and brilliant businessman—would harbor a preference for the sandy paths and formal geometry of imposing gardens in the classic French style. Not at all. His home, Le Mas Vincent, located at Saint-Rémy on the road to Saint-Paul-de-Mausole (the hospital where Van Gogh was treated after cutting off his ear) tells an entirely different story.

The dimensions of Bergé's property, extending behind a discreet cottage on a village street, are human in scale. When he first acquired it, the garden was no more than a patch of welcome shade. There was just enough room in it to set up a table under the trellis; he could throw open the shutters of the master-bedroom windows and look down onto a tiny courtyard with a linden tree and a Chinese mulberry at one end. Thrilled with the house's location—just a few steps from the center of town and the marketplace—Pierre Bergé commissioned Michel Sémini to design the garden, and architect Hugues Bosc to restore the cottage. He needed only a moment's thought in order to select two men as enthusiastic and determined as himself.

As promised, the work was finished the following summer. Meanwhile, the great poppy incident occurred. "I'd planted thirty olive trees on a carefully cleared strip of land," recounts Michel Sémini. "One morning, when I came out to see how they were doing, I found the field carpeted in red. Poppies sown by the wind! I called Pierre Bergé in Paris, and he rushed here to witness the miracle with his own eyes. He's repeated the story of the poppy incident all over the world."

Today Le Mas Vincent is a marvel of refinement and simplicity. Michel Sémini planted *Honeysuckle nitida* and *Pittosporum tenuifolium* around the trees in the courtyard, protecting them with low dry-stone walls. He added a marble doe that treads on a carpet of blue forget-me-nots on her way to drink at a fountain. Plane trees, palmettos, and white flowers in tubs separate the space into cool and intimate salons.

This little corner of paradise has been enlarged over the years, and now covers almost 6,500 square feet. Next to the olive grove, Hugues Bosc designed a view focused on a mirror pool. A Hellenic-inspired

The pool-side cabana takes the form of a Grecian pavilion. Opening onto the garden and roofed with red tiles in the traditional Mediterranean way, it is reflected in the blue waters of the pool. In the foreground, clumps of honeysuckle and pittosporum underscore the sensuality of the setting. An impression of well-being and serenity reigns in this graceful enclosed area designed by Michel Sémini.

Turning its back on the Palladian-style greenhouse where a collection of hibiscus plants is stored during the winter, an eighteenth-century terra-cotta statue of Neptune rises from a clump of reeds growing between two superb Medici urns. Armed with his trident, the sea god stands in the pool and vigilantly surveys his aquatic realm (facing page). A mass of Virginia creeper twining around columns and invading walls and ceiling transforms the pool pavilion into an elegant salon of greenery. Rustic garden furniture, Moroccan ceramics, and potted plants welcome Pierre Bergé's guests after a sunbathe or a plunge in the swimming pool (right, top). Cypress trees dot the alley leading to the Moroccan garden. A bench provides strollers with an opportunity to rest while admiring the marvels of Provençal nature (right, bottom).

summerhouse with Doric columns faces an eighteenth-century terra-cotta statue of Neptune standing in the water—a nod to Greek mythology. On the same axis, behind a field of lavender, a greenhouse protects fragile hibiscus plants from the rigors of the Provençal winter.

There are more surprises in store. A path edged with irises leads to the Moroccan garden, a spot reserved for friends with fond memories of the Majorelle garden in Marrakech. Sheltered by the fronds of semi-tropical plants, two elegantly exotic bedrooms open onto a patio where a fountain murmurs in the center of a mosaic pool.

Le Mas Vincent is an invitation to introspection and reverie. Its annex, Le Mas Théo, designed as an extension to the original house, also offers its share of magic. Fruits, vegetables, and flowers planted in orderly rows within a charming, old-fashioned, country-style garden face a trellis under which guests can pause for refreshment. It is here, in this enclosure forged by mind and hand, that Pierre Bergé revives his spirits and, with them, the memory of his childhood friend Jean Giono—the bard of an invincible and generous Provence from whom Bergé "learned about beauty, a taste for real things and real people."

Jean-Claude Brialy's secret garden

Glimpsed through the arched doorway of the orangery, the summer dining room invites family and friends to relax around the wrought-iron table in this shady nook (above). The owner of the house frequently convenes his guests for delectable luncheons and lively conversation on the terrace protected by a screened roof (facing page).

When Michel Sémini, who has designed some of the finest gardens in the Luberon and the foothills of the Alps, describes the garden he created below Les Baux-de-Provence for Jean-Claude Brialy, the celebrated film and theater actor, he mentions the surprise he felt when first viewing the property. The house, restored by Hugues Bosc, was charming; the garden much less so. This was just a small vacant lot measuring 650 square feet with a huge hen house in the middle; an unexceptional patch of land on which two cypress trees and a tall Aleppo pine were visibly languishing. The creation of a garden requires perfect empathy between landscape artist and owner, and Jean-Claude Brialy has a penchant for surprises planned against a meticulously organized backdrop. After touring the plot from one end to the other, Michel Sémini immediately set to work, designing a series of natural salons around a variety of viewpoints in order to create an illusion of depth—indulging in a game of outdoor building-blocks.

Nothing is more important to a man of the theater than grand entrances. Sémini did not have a curtain he could raise, so he designed a wooden door, painted blue and half-hidden in the shrubbery. Stepping over the threshold of this doorway, one is greeted by a stunning scene. First, a white gravel path bordered by round boxwood hedges and honeysuckle, shaded by a clump of bamboo, and leading to a little bower filled with rattan furniture.

The terrace jutting out from the house's blue-shuttered façade also offers an inviting resting-place under a trellis covered with wisteria and begonia. Across from this shady nook parallel to the house is a stone swimming pool with Anduze tubs of boxwood at each corner. On one side is a seat attached to an ivy-covered wall with a little fountain in it. The area reserved for swimming and sunbathing is framed by a low dry-stone wall. Three antique wrought-iron benches against a backdrop of olive groves echo the three palm trees casting their reflections into the tranquil waters of the pool. Placed at various spots around the garden are secret nooks, hidden by the shrubbery, perfect for taking a nap or reading.

Luncheon is served on the terrace, except when the weather is too warm or too cool. Guests then move into the orangery, built by Hugues Bosc, where Brialy has assembled a collection of unusual and quaint

Behind a bamboo grove, the master of the house has installed an Anduze urn next to a seat on which guests can savor, in silence, a good book, a short nap, or—why not?—simply a moment of solitude (far left, top). Standing on a low wall, a stone fruit basket, discovered at a local antique dealer's, tries to merge into its natural surroundings (far left, bottom). The deck chairs, arranged temptingly by the pool, invite sunbathers to admire this luxuriant and exotic setting in which palm trees vie with rose laurels for attention. For every carefully scheduled activity, there is a correspondingly specific scenario, a particular natural backdrop, and an appropriate ambience (left). A double row of trimmed lonicera separates the various salons of greenery that have been meticulously designed and installed by landscape architect Michel Sémini (right, above).

objects and furnishings. Each of the outdoor salons is furnished with a refined elegance that can adapt itself to different moments in the day. Both the house and the garden are as charming as their famous owner, and contrive to project a feeling of bucolic and poetic conviviality both inside and out—the whole is like a play with a happy ending that is both serious and lighthearted, tender and beguiling. One that can be relished even when one's eyes are shut.

A river of lavender winds
through a meadow,
tumbles down a hill, and
vanishes into a little lake
of grapevines; this is Alex
Dingwall-Main's tribute
to the Mediterranean
countryside (above).
Ducks roam freely in a
secluded corner, where this
landscape architect has
orchestrated a symphony
of greens, from the silvery
gray-tinged shades of olive
tree and santolina, to the
lustrous deeper tones of
pittosporum (right).

An English landscape architect in the Luberon

Alex Dingwall-Main, a landscape architect renowned on both sides of the Channel, is often asked, "Do you make English gardens?" His laconic reply, which fends off arguments and forces people to use their own eyes is, "No. I make gardens." Between Ménerbes and Bonnieux, below the ruins of the Marquis de Sade's château at Lacoste, Dingwall-Main found an old farm and decided to transform the land around it, which had been devastated by the uprooting of a vineyard, into a little corner of paradise.

Some 800 tons of earth, which had been excavated from the ground floor of the building, determined the configuration of the garden. Respecting the local concept of terraced fields, Dingwall-Main designed a slope linking the house to the sheer portion of the terrain. This succession of curves affords a sensual appearance to the land. To beguile the eye, he installed a mass of lavender that zigzags across a meadow toward a little "lake" of grapevines and spreads gracefully around a grove of wild quince trees. Other sources of visual pleasure are the stream of santolina cascading toward the house, and a grove of bamboo concealing a pond filled with water lilies.

Playfulness is a major feature of Dingwall-Main's garden. To amuse his son Théo, he planted a boxwood maze in the English stately-home tradition. He was fascinated by this project, which adds an element of risk to the pleasure of strolling through a complex geometrical design.

Inspired by the impressionists, Dingwall-Main's palette features a wide range of pinks and blues against a symphony of greens. He brings from his homeland a love of roses, which climb the walls, cover trellised arbors, and creep among the hedges.

There was one major problem: in a garden begun only four years ago, how can one create areas of shade? To imitate the effect of old plane trees and blackberry bushes, Dingwall-Main designed a series of terraces, planting them with bowers of shrubbery and rows of cypress trees. He also added scores of cherry trees that produce abundant white blooms in early spring and baskets of delicious fruit later on.

"My garden is not very chic," remarks Dingwall-Main, "but it's the kind of garden I prefer—a charming and delectable spot in which to taste the pleasures of living in Provence."

Glimpsed through the tempting fruit weighing down the branches of a cherry tree, an old farm once half-buried in the earth has recovered its former glory (above, top). A fig tree lends its shade to a little terrace prolonged by an arbor of greenery (above, bottom).

Alchemy in the garden

*This sixteenth-century manor with mysterious symbols on its walls was once the
home of alchemist Pierre Isnard, a friend and neighbor of Nostradamus (above).
The Mediterranean-style garden screening the fine stone manor house leads to another
garden, rich in surprises, designed as a journey of mystic initiation (right).*

At Eygalières near Saint-Rémy-de-Provence, two brilliant
landscape architects—Arnaud Maurières and Éric Ossart—have
designed a contemporary version of the alchemist's garden for
Alain and Marie de Larouzière, owners of Le Mas de la Brune. Partially
hidden by an alley of chestnuts, this charming manor house—embodying
all the architectural splendor of the sixteenth century—was built in 1572
for Pierre Isnard, consul to Eygalières. Isnard was an influential local official
fascinated by alchemy, as well as a neighbor of the notorious Nostradamus.
Today converted into a charming country hotel, Le Mas de la Brune still
bears on its façade, beside a languorous mermaid with a cleft tail, the
mysterious symbols of an occult science that has fascinated men and
women since the Middle Ages.

After a thorough study of plans drawn up by Renaissance agronome
Olivier de Serres, and repeated readings of treatises on alchemy, Arnaud
and Éric designed a garden-maze based on numerology and the secret
symbols of an arcane doctrine combining experimental chemistry with
mystic speculation. Leading up to the house is an avenue of cypress trees
protected by a row of white canvas curtains. Following the principles of
the Great Work, the Alchemy garden is divided into three parts: the Black
Work, the White Work, and the Red Work.

In the "black" garden, where darkness is obviously the keynote, cool
shade is created by rows of cypresses—trees associated with mourning
and sorrow and also, because of their evergreen foliage, with the notion
of immortality—and the still water in a square mirror-pool: the Fountain
of Knowledge. The color black also suggests lead, the symbolic Saturnine
element that alchemists attempted to transform into gold—a transmutation
as valid for the human spirit as for the base metal.

In the "white" garden, governed by the Moon, the symbolic substance
is mercury—a unique liquid metal essential for extracting gold. Here
white is projected by clumps of immaculate roses, representing monastic
wisdom; and lilies, heraldic symbols of glory and fertility. White is also
provided by a luminous marble path leading to a circular pool.

The last section, the "red" garden, represents the end of the alchemist's
quest, when the ultimate Work emerges from the preceding esoteric
experiments: the lead has been transmuted into gold; the alchemist has

Arnaud Maurières and Éric Ossart studied treatises on alchemy, applying what they learned to the design of their garden. Visitors enter the back garden, governed by the numeral 11, through a dark hedgerow leading to a black-gravel path, where pots of sharp-leafed ophiopogona are aligned in symbolic rows (facing page, top). Beyond, aeoniums with deep violet, almost black, leaves balance precariously in their pots (facing page, bottom). Cypress trees fronted by white curtains line the alley separating the Magic garden from the Alchemist's garden, which replicates the quest of scholars fascinated by the occult sciences (left). In the Magic garden, fences made from willow stems planted in a cross-hatch pattern protect herbs and shrubs native to the South of France, displaying the secrets of Provençal nature to visitors (right, above).

found the philosopher's stone or grasped the wingéd snake. The organization of this third garden is ruled by solar geometry. Scarlet roses blaze around a little pool in the shape of a seven-pointed star framed by pomegranate trees, their branches heavy with the fruit that is symbolic of fertility and plenty.

Tours of the Alchemy garden, which is open to the public, are usually preceded by a visit to the Magic garden, where Mediterranean herbs and plant species are planted inside square plots enclosed by willow trellises. Grapevines are honorably represented by twenty-two different root stocks. The collection, established on the basis of research conducted by ethno-botanist Pierre Lieuthaghi, includes the medicinal plants and herbs most frequently used in Provence. An exploration of these two gardens, symbolically separated by a curtain, unfolds like a mock initiation through which visitors hunt treasure and solve riddles. Do they understand, at its conclusion, that the end of the quest is the beginning of life?

A planetary garden at Le Rayol

On a fifty-acre seaside property designed to reflect the "exotic-travel" theme common to several great estates along the Côte d'Azur, a wide stone staircase bordered with gigantic cypress trees leads to the pergola (above), a graceful Art Deco structure built during the 1920s by banker Alfred Théodore Courmes.

When the French Coastal Conservation Commission purchased the Domaine du Rayol in 1989, renowned agricultural engineer and landscape architect Gilles Clément was commissioned to design the garden. The history of this domain forms part of the gilded and tormented legend of the Côte d'Azur. Before the First World War, banker Alfred Théodore Courmes bought a fifty-acre plot of land along the seaside near Le Lavandou on the Les Maures corniche—a wide hillside locked between two spurs of rock above a sandy beach. Courmes ordered the construction on his new acquisition of two houses in the architectural style of the period. The first, built in 1910, is a tribute to the sinuous curves of Art Nouveau; the second, completed in 1925, is designed in the streamlined Art Deco style. Sadly, following a reverse in his fortunes, Courmes later took his own life.

In 1940 the domain passed into the hands of Henri Potez, an aviation pioneer who dabbled in horticulture. Potez immediately hired some twenty gardeners and, following the taste for theme gardens that has been in vogue on the Côte d'Azur since the turn of the century, had them plant a series of terraces with tropical trees. Palm, carob, and citrus trees—plus a few South African species—resisted as best they could the depredations of inclement weather and neglect.

Gilles Clément, talented co-designer of the Citroën park, the gardens at the Abbaye de Valloires, l'Arche, Lazenay, and the Château de Blois—and renowned as well for his fascination with undeveloped land and his "gardens-in-motion" theory—proposed an unusual but logical plan for reviving the domain. After consulting with naturalist and botanist François Macquart-Moulin, Clément developed a theme derived from the typical Mediterranean garden. He then expanded on it, taking maximum advantage of the microclimate prevailing on the Le Rayol site. This explains the genesis of the South African, New Zealand, Chilean, Chinese, and Mexican gardens. A total of thirty-five acres display plants native to these regions, including mixed grasses, cistus, and wild meadow-flowers.

In a ravine already filled with natural growths of acanthus and white forget-me-nots, Clément planted arum lilies and bulbs. Near Le Figuier point he designed a seaside garden at the beach's edge; he is currently planning an underwater garden. Drawing on a deft interplay of shapes,

colors, and species, he has combined aloes with banana trees, purple-blooming polygalas, orange leonotis, and red-blooming callistemon.

The gem of the entire domain is, arguably, the vertical axis formed by a magnificent staircase lined with cypress trees and overlooked by a pergola dating from the 1920s. Visitors must settle the argument for themselves! Gilles Clément added a second staircase to the first, extending the axis still farther. This straight line, the only one in the garden, traverses the domain from end to end. Visitors should pause at the foot of the steps to admire the royal eucalyptus reigning supreme from the hilltop.

Although the domain of Le Rayol is the focus of continuous experimentation, respect is also maintained for the spirit and history of the site. This planetary "garden-in-motion" provides, undidactically, its share of insights and surprises to specialist and non-specialist alike, leading us on a voyage around the world. As if by magic!

"Gardens," notes Gilles Clément, perhaps alluding to this recent and constantly evolving creation, "are the only spaces in which human beings allow themselves to live out their dreams."

The magnificently orchestrated vertical axis of the garden can best be appreciated from the top of the staircase. Gilles Clément has added tropical species to native varieties, thus creating an impression of earthly paradise (above). Taking advantage of the coastal coves tucked between the rocks, he also built a beach hut for visiting scuba divers eager to explore the local aquatic flora (left).

Centuries-old olive trees with knotted trunks alternate with impeccably trimmed cypresses (above). The garden's central axis is marked by a converted irrigation basin, edged by white agapantha and pittisporum, and with huge Cretan jars at each corner. Adding a cool, refreshing note, the pool dominates the sloping land, suspended as if by magic above the gulf of Saint-Tropez (right).

An Eden overlooking Saint-Tropez

On the beach road above Saint-Tropez, Louis Benech has created a magical setting in a garden descending gently toward the Mediterranean Sea. At the extreme tip of the property, shimmering in the sunlight above the treetops, is a scene that appears to come straight out of a Paul Signac painting: the pink-tiled roofs of a little fishing village stand etched against the blue sea. A remark by the author Colette comes to mind: "Saint-Tropez belongs to those who rise at dawn." This is certainly true of Louis Benech's garden. It should ideally be seen at dawn, when pearly dew-drops glisten on white agapanthus blooms and the sun's early rays gently caress the lawns before moving on to the foliage above.

This naturally sloping Saint-Tropez garden, which is surrounded by vineyards, was designed to harmonize with the natural landscape. At the foot of the house Benech has built a series of small patios and filled them with tropical plants. Palmettos and Washingtonia palms share the limited space available with an albizia, daturas, and borders of headily fragrant pittosporum.

In the rear, between the house and a magnificent vegetable garden hidden by a hedge of bay trees, Anduze tubs filled with plumbagos are dotted around a swimming pool, which inscribes its bright blue against a background of greenery. An arbor laden with wisteria, bougainvillea, and Virginia creeper provides swimmers with inviting shade.

This is an enchanting spot, but the real excitement is in front of the house. Taking his cue from the region's terraced fields, Louis Benech has divided the front garden into lengthwise sections beginning at the top of the property. Hundred-year-old olive trees underscored by two rows of pomegranates protect the lower, "lady's garden," a space designed with daring and formal discipline—a geometrical arrangement of artichokes, lantanas, and peach trees.

The garden's central section, which appears to plunge downward toward the harbor, is organized around an old irrigation basin which has been converted into a mirror pool. This pool, bordered with agapanthus and iris, is the focus for various sight-lines. Two paths lead to the house: one bordered with Greek friezes and a skillful arrangement of boxwood and myrsinaceae; the other featuring a subtle range of blue tones. For his

Composed like an impressionist painting by Monet, Cross, or Signac, the pathway running up to the house is edged in blue shades ranging from pale azure to deep indigo; the refined blend includes species both common and rare—a subtle interplay of thistle, perovskia, verbena, sage, agathaean, and campanula.

Agapanthas are reflected in the still waters of a mirror-pool (left). On the other side of the house, a second garden has been planted around the swimming pool. A superb vegetable garden and a few grapevines are concealed behind the stately parasol pine that rises above a laurel hedge. Anduze urns filled with plumbagoes are dotted around the pool, echoing its geometric shape, and accenting the contrasting interplay of blue and green (right). Near the entrance, a profusion of tropical plants are mirrored in a minuscule ornamental pond (facing page, top). Louis Benech has designed a private garden for the mistress of the house that is unusually daring: echoing the shades featured in the main garden, patches of alternating colors are planted with artichokes, lantanas, and peach trees (facing page, bottom).

"blue" path, Louis Benech combined wild species—thistle, for example—with more sophisticated ones, such as perovskia, verbena, sage, agathaean, and campanula.

Paths named according to their style and color fan out from the central pool. The "yellow" path is a luminous festival of Saint John's wort and senna; this leads to a summer house conveniently furnished with a bench—a romantic and aromatic hideaway filled with blooms of the incredible solandra. The "white" path is lined with laurel and lilac trees interspersed with Iceberg and Mont-Blanc roses. Another path, "the palms," leads strollers into an imaginary Orient filled with tropical species such as the albizia, with its bright red, feather-light blooms. They then follow a shady path leading back to the house, which boasts a wealth of bamboo varieties barely discernible in the shadows. Finally, they might linger for a moment by the camellias before emerging onto the central path and returning to their point of departure, dazzled by the contrast between the rigor of the garden's design, the subtlety of its chromatic color range, and the profusion of its plant species.

Are all visitors able to recognize the michelia or the *Tetra arborea*, which are two of Louis Benech's favorite plants? Probably not, but none will ever forget the vision of this garden of Eden suspended above the gulf of Saint-Tropez.

MYTHICAL GARDENS

A few famous gardens that are open to the public have stories to tell—some lighthearted, some serious. The story played out on the terrace of the Château de Barbentane is a baroque drama. At the Villa Noailles garden in Hyères, it's a cubist painting that awaits you. At Les Colombières, Val Rahmeh, and the Villa Maria Serena in Menton, it's the whisper of an exotic fragrance. Some gardens—Entrecasteaux or Ansouis, for example—reflect a pronounced taste for outward show; others emphasize the simple country life. While at the Château de la Gaude between Aix and Marseilles, visitors are invited by nature and the master of the house to share in a secret celebration.

A garden in a vineyard on the banks of the Durance

Justly famed for the excellence of its wines, the Château de Val Joanis is also renowned for its old-fashioned vegetable garden, restored by the owner and planted like an ornamental garden (preceding double page). The courtyard is paved with pebbles from the Durance river and refreshed by a cool fountain (above). A long arbor covered with antique roses connects the house to the vineyard (facing page).

The Val Joanis gardens lie at the heart of a wine-growing property covering some 500 acres, located near Pertuis on the Cavaillon road, where they surround a sixteenth-century farmhouse. The present owner is Cécile Chancel, who is a passionate gardener, eminent botanist, and graduate of one of the world's foremost landscape-architecture schools, The Chelsea English Gardening School. At Val Joanis, she has drawn on horticultural treatises and her own intuition in order to redesign the gardens.

A brisk tour of the property in the company of Cécile progresses from terrace to terrace, and then through the newly replanted ornamental vegetable garden. It is a marvelous experience, rich in lessons learned from the late Tobie Loup de Viane, a great creator of gardens, as well as the more contemporary concepts of Philippe Déliau. It also incorporates an idea suggested by Louis Benech: the planting of a sumptuous alley of olive trees leading to the vineyard.

Protected by a charming paved courtyard, the farmhouse opens onto a ground-floor terrace shaded by tall Aleppo pines. On the land below, Tobie Loup de Viane has designed an Italian garden ornamented with boxwood hedges and santolina borders; these are punctuated by large Medici vases. The lower terrace holds a swimming pool of straightforward design, which is surrounded by brick-colored beach umbrellas. On the same level, a small house with a glazed-tile roof offers a cool spot in which bathers can change. A shady garden beyond the knoll is filled with bamboo and native plant species.

However, Cécile Chancel's greatest efforts have gone into the old-fashioned vegetable garden, which she has transformed from one end to the other. Medieval-style willow fences now alternate with borders of lavender and aromatic herbs punctuated by knobs of boxwood. The rows of squash, artichokes, spinach, and tomato vines are tended attentively. Because of their color, some vegetables—beans and Swiss chard, for example—are even used ornamentally. So are the fruit trees, planted in rows or pruned in the palmetto style to show off their graceful geometry, as recommended by Jean de La Quintinie, gardener to Louis XIV.

The pool overlooking this unusual and bucolic composition affords a view of the summerhouse at the center of a rectangle edged with

An alley of centuries-old olive trees designed by Louis Benech leads to the vineyards, object of loving care on the part of Jean-Louis Chancel. The AOC (Appellation d'Origine Contrôlée) Côtes du Luberon wines produced by the Val Joanis vineyards are frequent prize-winners (facing page, top). An olive grove flooded with deep-blue lavender (facing page, bottom). The old-fashioned kitchen garden, in which both native and exotic varieties of vegetable are planted ornamentally among rose bushes and aromatic herbs, is a creation of Cécile Chancel's fertile imagination (left). The lower terrace is reserved for relaxation—alfresco lunches, swimming, and sunbathing (right, top). Under a brick-red parasol, Cécile Chancel welcomes her guests with a few good bottles of Val Joanis wine and delectable dishes made by her own expert hand (right, bottom).

ornamental yews. These are trimmed in conical shapes and appear vividly etched against the blue sky. After crossing a bed of iris ranging in color from white to indigo, the path leads back to the house, passing under a long hedgerow of old-fashioned tango-orange roses.

"Bright orange may be considered vulgar," explains the mistress of the house, "but I love it because it's so cheerful. I also like the striped roses I learned about from the great specialist André Eve." Chancel, who travels worldwide in her search for seeds, explains: "I designed the garden in nineteen eighty-two. We used Roman stone for the dividing walls. We decided on two planting periods annually over four years, using four thousand to five thousand seedlings each time. The famous Schneider sisters' nursery in Cannes was very helpful."

Cécile Chancel is just as proud of her blue path—with its medley of nepetas, caryopteris, perovskias, and vitex—as she is of her cabbage and potato patches. She describes her gardens with wit and enthusiasm as "a vast organized disorder that perfectly suits the way we live." Without being ostentatious, Val Joanis manages to express a particularly infectious joie de vivre through the harmony of its colors and forms and the luxuriance of its vegetation.

The heritage of a great landscape artist

Lawrence Johnston's hilltop house overlooks terraced gardens and a succession of staircases descending toward a mirror-pool (above). Johnston, an eminent landscape architect, designed terraces affording magnificent views that alternate with secluded areas and feature an interplay of shade and sunlight (facing page).

Before taking the Gorbio road to Menton and venturing onto the mossy paths of La Serre de la Madone—a legendary garden acquired by the French Coastal Conservation Commission in 1999—it might be advisable, first, to visit Hidcote Manor in England. These two historic gardens have something important in common: the man who designed them, Lawrence Johnston. An American by birth, Cambridge Univeristy-graduate Johnston was an early twentieth-century gentleman farmer who, between 1924 and 1958, took a dream first nourished in the cold mists of Gloucestershire and made it come true in the land of the orange blossom.

During his travels around the globe, this inveterate wanderer and eccentric botanist amassed a huge collection of rare plants, particularly ligneous ones. He brought specimens too fragile for the Cotswold Hills to La Serre de la Madone, planting them in small garden plots. Johnston's passion for exotic species is movingly reflected by the *Stenocarpus sinuatus,* which flowers every ten years, two impressively tall yellow-woods, and the Asian magnolias framing the gate. Today, visitors strolling under an arbor heavy with Japanese wisteria will no doubt pause to imagine what this splendid garden might have looked like in former times, when it was tended by a dozen gardeners.

This geometrically designed neo-rural English garden is a skillful blend of the rigid and the natural. Johnston replicated a very formal design for the central section of his garden and then, cavalierly turning his back on the sparkling Mediterranean below, divided the rest of the sloping terrain into terraces that merge into the landscape around them. Seven of the fifteen acres forming the total area of the property display a "calculated alternation between the expected and the unexpected," as noted by Nigel Nicolson, son of diplomat Sir Harold Nicolson and Vita Sackville-West, the English novelist who created the famed gardens at Sissinghurst.

Lawrence Johnston designed outdoor "green rooms," framed a shady garden in the French style with groves of shrubbery, and built a vividly colored oriental patio that was greatly admired by all of his guests. The latter were inevitably asked to follow an immutable ceremony, climbing a steep twisting path to the orangery on an upper terrace where Johnston

Opposite the orangery, a central path runs down the middle of a double mirror-pool that plays host to a collection of lotus and papyrus. This somewhat nostalgic aquatic setting recalls the golden age of Côte d'Azur gardens and is the most romantic spot at La Serre de la Madone, especially in autumn, when fallen leaves—irresistible reminders of fleeting time—cover the paths. A graceful eighteenth-century statue, nicknamed "Mrs. Johnston," and draped in sunlight and her own dignity, is reflected in the green waters of the pool (left). Lotus and water-lilies vie with each other in beauty and delicacy; their flowers open only at certain times of the day to reveal the iridescent corollas within (right, top). Pots of citrus trees on the pool's edge are well protected from the weather and bear silent witness to the benefits of Menton's microclimate (far right).

had a surprise in store for them: a romantic vision, a water garden filled with lotus and papyrus that is guarded by a majestic female figure draped in a Roman-style toga of stone. Could this be the famed Madonna of La Serre? Or is it an effigy representing the lady of the house, Mrs. Johnston? Judge for yourself!

Visitors following this path today are rewarded for their efforts with plenty of surprises. To reach the Provençal palazzo built onto an old farmhouse, they climb a series of single and double landings and staircases imitating those found in Italian Renaissance gardens. Will they halt in front of the two mysterious sphinxes guarding the steps? Will they pause near the fountain in the Moorish patio, linger in the Tangerine Tree courtyard? If they are observant, they will note the vestiges of an old aviary formerly inhabited by macaws, ibises, cranes, and golden pheasants. They may visualize the beauty of acacias, yuccas, and peony shrubs displaying double blooms; of cool pergolas and grottoes. With just a little imagination and intuition, they will let themselves be drawn onward, from closed to open space, yielding to the pleasure of a journey that sometimes leads them through what look like tropical forests.

The gardens at La Serre de la Madone are currently being restored. By 2003, their original splendor will be visible again and the famed collections of bulbs and herbaceous plants should once more be on display. However, even now, with the work as yet not completed, the gardens contrive to retain a charm that wafts over the paths like a heady perfume.

Water on display in the heart of Provence

A majestic alley of plane trees (above) stands in the "upper garden;" they were planted in about 1850 to replace the original elms. The alley runs along the banks of a 260-foot long canal, and is emblematic of the Provençal method for taming rivers. At the far end of the canal, a cool grotto covered with seashells and chalk deposits evokes the fashion for Italian-style follies (facing page).

These two gardens located at Bouc-Bel-Air (on the Marseilles road, seven miles from Aix-en-Provence) were designed in 1751 by the Marquis Jean-Baptiste d'Albertas, first president of the Cours des Comptes d'Aix-en-Provence and a man fascinated with horticulture. The gardens were intended to serve as the showcase for a ravishing château to be built later.

Before embarking on this project, Jean-Baptiste d'Albertas had divided his time between a luxurious private town house in Aix-en-Provence and the Château de Gémenos. While the gardens were being installed, he often stayed at the charming hunting lodge he had erected as a temporary residence on the site. It was common practice at the time to plan the garden first, and then create the house. However, the marquis became so obsessed with his gardens that the house was never built. Jean-Baptiste d'Albertas was assassinated in 1790 at Gémenos. The two French gardens he left behind—still intact today—are the region's finest ornament, and the most accomplished surviving examples of eighteenth-century Provençal garden design.

The two gardens, each protected by an imposing gate, face each other on either side of a road that (oddly) runs between them. The lower section, or "Jardin d'en Bas," features a fine alley of cedars and a stone pool ornamented with large Medici vases. The hunting lodge, converted between 1764 and 1767 by architect Laurent-Alexandre Vallon, is today the country home of the d'Albertas family's descendants.

Heralded majestically by a wrought-iron gate bearing the d'Albertas coat-of-arms, the "Jardin d'en Haut" is a delight for strollers. Visitors follow a main alley lined on both sides with chestnut trees and leading to a grand canal decorated with twelve bestiary masks. The walk continues toward a cool grotto, and then on to the "pool of seventeen fountains," a marvel of hydraulic engineering once fed by water from five springs. Here, water—a rare commodity in Provence—has been given a dramatic role, emphasizing the wealth of the property's owner. The weight of a terrace in the center of the pool is supported by atlantes, their efforts encouraged by chubby little tritons blowing into conch shells. This stage-like terrace was designed to serve as a gallery for antique sculpture: informed visitors will recognize a "Borghese" gladiator with raised fist;

The "upper garden" is strongly influenced by Versailles and the great formal French gardens. Here, elaborate display is the keynote. Marble statues of mythological heroes play starring roles on a terrace supported by colossal atlantes, or carved male figures, against an ordered backdrop of mathematically designed paths. An Italian influence is also evident at Albertas. The garden's spectacular alternations of light and shadow, the majesty of its trees and the exceptional width and depth of its flower beds, are all enhanced by the role of water here— which is appreciated for its fluid motion, burbling music, and mirror effects (left). Frozen marble statues of virile and warlike Greek heroes, identifiable by their respective poses and weapons, gaze down on chubby Tritons blowing jets of cool water through their conch shells into the pool below (right, above).

a David adjusting his sling; a Greek gladiator drawing his sword; and a Hercules (behind them), exhausted by his labors but proud of having vanquished the Nemean lion, rubbing three apples from the Garden of the Hesperides with one hand.

The ideal time for a visit to Albertas is the last Sunday in May, for the Festival of Rare and Mediterranean Plants. The festival includes displays by some sixty distinguished exhibitors and a program of special events featuring renowned landscape architects. Visitors will not fail to be impressed, at the same time, by the spectacle presented in both upper and lower gardens. They will be dazzled by the elegance of the setting, the splendor of the views, the interplay of pools and statuary. And yet, should they spare a thought for the cruel destiny of life, they might also sense a hint, in the gardens of Albertas, of a charming and languorous melancholy.

INTERIORS

A PLACE IN THE SUN

*The Château de Sainte-Roseline, a former fourteenth-century abbey, was
completely rebuilt by architect Jean-Michel Wilmotte. The contemporary bias is reflected
in the clean lines of the furniture in the master bedroom (preceding double page).
Françoise and Bernard Teillaud, the proprietors of this prestigious wine-growing estate,
have retained traces of the past—such as this boxwood maze—in their garden (above).
Behind the centuries-old plane trees that frame a stone pool, Anduze urns filled with
boxwood are ranged along the façade of the house (facing page).*

Provence is eternal. The cottages and farmhouses known locally as *mas* and *bastides* still evoke dreams of bliss amid the vineyards or under a shady plane tree. But something has changed. Today's architects are offering a fresh image of the way in which these dreams should be realized. Cypress trees, olive groves, and even vineyards are safe in the hands and imaginations of these contemporary artists—whether they come from the North or the South—who express a newfound respect for the landscape. They are all directing their efforts toward the integration of their designs into the natural surroundings; all are applying lessons learned from their predecessors in order to protect buildings from the mistral, modulate the sunlight, and exploit the best natural exposures. Although some of the new architectural concepts may be radical—at times just an unadorned parallelogram built into a hillside, or a cube of glass and wood nestled in a forest of evergreen oak and pine—they are designed to preserve the local topography, and thus to blend seamlessly into their surroundings.

Modern architecture, as demonstrated by Jean-Michel Wilmotte at the Château Sainte-Roseline, represents a continuous dialogue between interior and exterior. This fourteenth-century former abbey, altered over succeeding centuries, is today a major wine-producing domain in the Var. Wilmotte immersed himself in the property's spirit, history, and function—grafting onto the old structure a streamlined design now serving as a showcase for a remarkable collection of contemporary art.

A constant feature of Provençal lifestyles is the interplay between house and garden. Terraces fall into a category of their own. Never treated as an afterthought, the terrace is generally the most convivial spot on the property, sometimes conditioning the very structure of the house. The swimming pool is also special. Traditionally a component of the garden, it comes into its own as a narrow strip for bathing that also plays a part in underscoring the architectural lines of the house. According to this approach, every structural component is a contrapuntal note contributing to the harmony of an overall esthetic principle. Despite the complaints of those who oppose modernity in every form, contemporary architecture—through the work of contemporary architects—has actually become a champion of the environment. This crucial point is, in fact,

a major argument passionately advanced by Rudy Ricciotti, Antonino Cascio, Christophe Petitcollot, Luc Svetchine, and most of their peers.

This intimate raport between nature and architecture, combining pleasure and utility, explains the delight of living in a *mas* or a *bastide*. These farmhouses originally defined themselves by their relation with a land that was not always generous and could only be mastered through effort and patience. Even when modernized, they cannot do without shady plane trees, an alley bordered with olive trees, or a modest vegetable garden. And nature is still a decisive presence around the *mas* or *bastide*. Houses in superb isolation appear to turn their backs on vineyard or olive grove, their façades opening freely onto gardens in the French style. Life in these *mas* and *bastides* has changed little over time. Contemporary lifestyles, however—although still ruled by sunlight and shade—combine two harmoniously coexisting approaches. First, the influence of oriental

(ie., Zen) philosophy; and, second, a desire to shed the superfluous and return to basics, expressed through respect for a house's original design, the original color of its walls and floors, and a taste for natural materials—fabric, wood, terra-cotta, wrought iron.

The same approaches are applied to houses clustered under village ramparts. Their interior decoration is dictated by tiled staircases and oddly shaped rooms with exposed beams and sloping ceilings. Today's new occupants must invent ingenious methods to improve their physical comfort while also preserving the spirit of their house. Sometimes a rooftop terrace is added, on which wisteria and bougainvillea play starring roles. Nature is ever-present, even in the stone universe at the heart of fortified villages. The dialogue between house and garden continues in historic homes, where—domesticated—it adds an embroidery of flower beds to the elegance of the façade, slips through the salon windows and imposes itself on the greenery of a tapestry. In the Alpine foothills, as in the Var, the Luberon, and on the Côte d'Azur, living the good life is more important than etiquette. Salons shed their formality and dining rooms feature daring decorative experiments that beguile guests. Shade is sought behind slatted shutters and beside fountains where the same age-old dilemma must be resolved: whether piously to preserve a setting that evokes the glorious past, or to opt for modernity. There is a third way: inventive compromise; a discerning selection of the best from both worlds.

Provence also represents freedom. The freedom to sling a hammock between two trees or build a little cabin. Shacks are erected for a season in cedar forests by the sea, put together with anything that comes to hand; they invite nature inside and revive the spirit of adventure. Cabins and shacks turn the ephemeral into poetry and—due to their unconventional appearance and improvised interior decoration—encourage occupants to be relaxed, friendly, and outgoing. And yet, the life lived in all of these contexts is much the same. With the exception of villa-museums prolonging the dreams of a few eccentrics and the extravagance of the Roaring Twenties, the interplay of shade and sunlight, the rhythm of the advancing day, are the same for all. The gales of laughter heard during a family lunch resound with as much good cheer on a château terrace as before the door of a seaside shack. To occupy a house in Provence is to recover the soul of childhood for the span of a summer holiday—or a lifetime. A house in Provence is a promise of happiness!

Jean-Michel Wilmotte designed the furniture for the Château Saint-Roseline dining room, which adjoins the kitchen (facing page). The staircase is built obliquely into the foyer, harmonizing with its stone setting (above, top).

In the little sitting room, white sofas designed by Antonio Citterio flank an eighteenth-century fireplace. A mysterious figure by Jean-Charles Blais seems to engage in silent dialogue with a statue of Buddha (above, bottom).

CONTEMPORARY INTERIORS

*F*or the architects working in today's world, a house is a fascinating canvas on which they can experiment, presenting a chance to explore many and varied possibilities. Materials, light, and geometry are the major components of constructions that are sometimes grafted onto older structures. A purity of line, a fluidity of space, a harmony of form, and an elegance of detailing redefine the architectural heritage of tomorrow.

Blue horizon near Toulon

It is perfectly possible to graft modern design seamlessly onto an old house, as the architect Rudy Ricciotti has demonstrated. Ricciotti is the much admired force behind the Bridge of Peace in Seoul, South Korea, as well as exhibition galleries at Paris's National Photography Center, and other prestigious contemporary designs. He was commissioned to convert a house near the Mourillon corniche above the port of Toulon. He recalls that when he first set eyes on the house it reminded him of Le Corbusier's seaside cabin and its esthetic functionalism based on a geometric structure with reinforced-concrete floors and walls, "a brutal, unflinching, dynamic material." For this young architect, the act of creation must address exterior reality, which he regards as the sole valid source of inspiration. Today, the Toulon villa, which has been completely redesigned by Rudy Ricciotti, offers a new perspective on modern architecture, proving it can indeed be perfectly integrated into the Provençal landscape.

Built against a rocky bluff overlooking the Mediterranean, the all-new extension, which has been added to the existing traditional construction, is reflected in a narrow sea-blue swimming pool designed like a rectangular ninety-foot stream. Two oaks with gnarled trunks lean toward the water and shade the lunch table. At night, with the help of expert lighting, the oaks etch a counterpoint of mysterious graphic symbols against the straight lines of the pool.

The architect's approach to the project draws on a series of logical contrasts, a dialogue between empty and full that shows to full advantage the carefully organized spaces. Chalk and powdered-marble walls echo the unfinished poured-concrete pillar and ceiling. African iroko-wood flooring, in the same blond color as the dry-stone wall enclosing the terrace, runs throughout the house. In the salon, a luminous ray of light running along the wooden floorboards underscores the strict geometry of the room's design.

The streamlined white-on-white furniture—the tables and chairs are by Philippe Starck—appears to float in space, defying the laws of gravity. The sole touch of color is a small jade-green side table by Ettore Sottsass; the only curved line is a sinusoid bookcase by Ron Arad. By contrast, furnishings with an organic slant—a table by Oscar Tusquets and armchairs

Adapting itself to a contemporary esthetic, the spirit of this villa has evolved. A glass-and-concrete wing added to the original structure follows the topography of the terrain, while the balcony is a reminder of the past (preceding double page). Rebuilt by Rudy Ricciotti, this house, overlooking the crystal-clear waters of a cove, proves that modern architecture can harmonize perfectly with the shores of the Mediterranean (above).

Cultivating a minimalist spirit through rigorously white furnishings in organic shapes, the salon opens onto the terrace. There, the narrow swimming pool has been built parallel to it and forming a right-angle with the old dry-stone wall (above). Through the windows of the owners' upper-floor bedroom unfolds a magical view, in which the sea and the flat roof have star billing (right).

by Starck—seem right at home under the dining room's ancient exposed beams. The dining room, like the kitchen, serves as a transition between the old part of the house and the modern extension. A staircase with luminous steps leads to the upper floor, where the minimalist approach is maintained by the almost monastic furnishings. Above the salon, the all-white master bedroom with a sea view framed by evergreen oaks and arbutus opens onto a terrace prolonged by a purple carpet of vervain. There are no drapes, just sheer curtains that have been hung from fishing rods to filter the sunlight.

"It's a paradisiacal spot," Rudy Ricciotti never tires of pointing out. "You're so steeped in views of the Mediterranean sea and countryside, you can almost believe that God is looking at you." Along this strip of coastline—which is still undeveloped, fortunately—the villa and swimming pool follow the topology of the terrain and merge into the local vegetation. Nature and architecture coexist in perfect harmony. Everything champions the cause of rationality and modernity, and its rigor here is synonymous with elegance.

The dining room unites past and present under the original exposed beams of its ceiling. Opening onto the terrace and the swimming-pool area, this room fosters the coexistence of two styles: traditional Provençal (through its structure), and contemporary (through its furnishings). The luxuriant greenery visible through windows on two sides of the room eliminates the need for paintings or wall decorations (above).

Hilltop transparencies

On a plot of land that is still semi-wild, spectacular trees and the use of wood and glass in the house's design reinforce an almost fusional relationship between architecture and nature. The alternation of stone walls painted brick-red with the house's transparent glass façade create contrasting harmonies between the opaque and the transparent, the full and the empty (above).

The hilly countryside above Saint-Paul-de-Vence, a stone's throw from the Mediterranean, is still wild and untouched. It is precisely this aspect of untamed nature that appealed to Antonino and Renée Cascio. They built their house on a sloping plot of land invaded by evergreen oaks and Aleppo pines. Antonino, a graduate of the Palermo School of Architecture and a worthy heir to the cult of formal beauty, is an impassioned advocate of modernity. His house is a wood-and-glass cube with a pitched roof, perfectly adapted to the terrain.

In order to underscore the integration of house and environment, Cascio used iroko (an African teak) for framing the glass panels. The walls were built using stones found on the site, and covered with brick-red paint made from natural pigments. The house is reached by a perfectly straight wooden ramp that appears to cut a path through the wilderness around it. An imposing tree placed midway along the ramp is a symbol denoting the central axis, as planned by the architect, that bisects house and garden.

The design of the house, which is set squarely on the landscape surrounding it, is best understood from the outside. Its light yet powerful plan is underscored by the main lines of the structure, which supports a row of metal pillars.

The wooded landscape visible through the picture windows of the main salon creates a poetic and natural atmosphere—a Mediterranean version of the Scandinavian style in which everyday life reflects a continuous dialogue between nature and architecture. The African teak parquet used for floors and terrace are sealed with rubber as they would be on the deck of a ship. In the same nautical spirit, the steel mesh on the railings of the upper-floor balcony resembles the netting of a hammock. Visitors, standing on the terrace or inside an upper-floor room, feel almost as though they are making a motionless cruise through the forest.

In the main living area, design classics including armchairs by Le Corbusier, Herbst, and Iosa Ghini, plus a table by Gae Aulenti, provide an additional note of modernity to the house's geometrical shape and the oblique line of its staircase. The rectangular fireplace and the

The occupants of the house spend most of their time on the terrace, which is like the bridge of a ship. Breakfast and afternoon tea are served in this informal salon, beside the pine tree growing at a slant under the sky-lit roof extension (left). The large windows and glass door of the kitchen afford a splendid view of the natural surroundings (above).

In the sunny main salon, contemporary furnishings fit harmoniously into a spacious and uncluttered area. The work of major twentieth-century designers is displayed against a backdrop of the forest outside. This fusion of nature and architecture does not preclude elegance, however. The African iroko parquet flooring used for both salon and terrace underscores the concept of continuity between interior and exterior. A giant alocasia, vying with a ficus by the window, seems to grow as we watch (left). A sculptural staircase connects the salon to the upper floor, where the building's main entrance is located. A collection of terra-cotta pieces from the Middle East and a Dogon door are displayed beneath a large picture window (right, above).

triangular painting by Claude Viallat that hangs nearby succeed in emphasizing the geometrical mood of the house without creating an impression of coldness.

The use of wood, the profusion of trees outside, the design of the house and arrangement of its rooms all contribute to a mood of intimacy and a relationship of virtual fusion with benevolent nature. The kitchen, its counter framed against sandstone tile and bleached-oak paneling, is supremely functional yet elegant. Functional elegance is also the keynote in the bathrooms, where raw lava is combined with wood paneling. By day as by night, light sculpts every space and enhances the ubiquitous transparency of the glass. In the evening, when subtle lighting works its magic and the luminous globes on the terrace could almost be mistaken for full moons, this house in the woods becomes a fairy-tale palace.

A work by Peter Klasen
delivers its disturbing
message in the
entranceway (above).
In the main living area,
the glass walls and doors
that run from floor to
ceiling offer an
unobstructed view of the
swimming pool and of
Peter's studio, visible
in counterpoint on the
other side of the lawn.
A collection of African
art and contemporary
furniture emphasizes
the elegant austerity of
this house (right).

Geometrical abstraction in the home of Peter Klasen

The artist Peter Klasen lives and works in Grasse during the summer months. Ever since the 1960s, Klasen's radically original esthetic vocabulary has made him one of the foremost members of the New Figuration movement. It is to this concept of geometric abstraction—honed since his student days at the Berlin School of Fine Arts—that he returned, in conjunction with architect Christophe Petitcollot, for the overall planning of this house. Completed in 1990, it is ideally situated on a hill overlooking the Vallée du Loup, which lies at the heart of the Grasse countryside below.

The sloping plot chosen for construction of the white structure designed by the two men is divided into even and harmonious terraced fields. "The 'words' forming the vocabulary that links a project to its site are points, lines, and shapes," explains the architect responsible for an overall design that is both rigorous and innovative.

The gate to the property is a discreet tribute to Charles Rennie Mackintosh. Beyond it, visitors are faced with an open construction site. However, if they continue along a diagonal line, they soon arrive at a cluster of flat-roofed buildings with the harmonious proportions and open sides characteristic of Greek temples. Every component in this cluster—main house, studio, gatekeepers' cottage, swimming pool—is perfectly square or rectangular.

The façades of the different buildings are regularly punctuated with narrow floor-to-ceiling glass panels that let in the light from outside. "But light is geometry!" claim artist and architect alike. The impressive height of the ceiling and the whiteness of the walls contrast with the granite floor and offset its heaviness. The dramatic foyer emphasizes vertical lines echoed by an antique ladder, granary door, and three shields from Cameroon. Within this immaculate space float a sculptural Nimba mask and seven-foot Dogon ritual-dance masks, their pictorial power balancing two large paintings by Klasen. Although skillfully controlled, empty space plays a crucial role here, whereas the center of the house is occupied—paradoxically—by a solid object: a concrete pillar that adds overwhelming dynamic tension to the area.

The rigor of the structure designed by the architect reflects the lifestyle of its owners. Klasen's wife is a renowned designer who presents

The dining room, which is an extension of the living room at one end of the house, is guarded by a wooden Bozo statue. Here we find four little square tables, designed by Peter Klasen, surrounded with chairs by Philippe Starck. The tables all have enigmatic messages on them: double arrows that may point nowhere, but that definitely take us off the beaten path (above).

her work under the name Claudine d'Hellemmes. For the living room she designed sofas, chairs, and a coffee table in highly streamlined, rectilinear shapes. In the teak-floored office, two Noguchi lamps cast their light over a reclining bed covered in black leather. Guests will find the comfortable red armchair designed by Gérard Van den Berg perfect for a moment's meditation while gazing at the neatly raked Zen garden outside and the two tree-sculptures it contains.

The dining room, perfect for convivial gatherings, is furnished with four square tables and a set of contrasting chairs. The room is an ideal vantage-point from which to view the tower-terrace, which connects the upper floor to the bedrooms. For the decor on this floor, Claudine chose a Japanese style, featuring multiple contrasting black-and-white graphic designs. A metallic staircase leads from the ground-floor to the tower, and is emblematic of the designer's need for isolation and height; the area up here becomes—depending on the time of day—a solarium or an ideal observation post. The tower is hollow and open to the elements; it extends the architectonic homogeneity of the façade while at the same time eliminating the need for unsightly balconies. It heightens the purity of the building's lines, etching its own dynamic rigor against the blue sky with jubilation and a perfect harmony.

Basing his design on a series of diagonals, architect Christophe Petitcollot placed Peter's studio and the gatehouse on an oblique axis, forming an angle with the horizontal lines of the terraced lawn (left, top). The functional kitchen, decorated in blue and black, continues the house's geometric spirit. Chromed steel is used for the hood over the stove and the burners (left, bottom). A Zen mood reigns in the master bedroom. In this serene setting, black and white are elegantly combined. The horizontal lines of the bed, covered in a white fabric with a calligraphy pattern, contrasts with the vertical line of the ladder (facing page). The bedroom is reached from the ground floor by way of an iron spiral staircase in the corridor (far right, top). A staircase with blue steps, dominated by a large Dogon shield, leads to the mezzanine (far right, bottom).

A focus on contemporary art

*On a rocky promontory at Saint-Jean-Cap-Ferrat, architect Luc Svetchine has succeeded
in integrating a pure and uncompromising architecture, inspired by Le Corbusier and
Mies van der Rohe, with the dry local terrain on which only a few evergreen oaks,
Aleppo pines, and thorn bushes grow. This contrast between mineral and organic
generates a vision that is dynamic and harmonious.*

Even on the fabled Riviera coastline, few spots are truly the stuff of which dreams are made. But the peninsula of Saint-Jean-Cap-Ferrat, one of the most sought-after sites on the Côte d'Azur, is just such a spot. From the nineteenth century onward, numerous celebrities from the worlds of finance and the performing arts have chosen it as their home and highly discreet refuge. Perched on a rocky promontory concealed from view, this villa is the joint work of two extremely talented men—architect Luc Svetchine and interior architect Frédéric Méchiche—who have often pooled their efforts for the realization of grandiose projects.

Perfectly integrated into a rocky terrain that is also covered with rampant Mediterranean underbrush, the villa's location is exceptional: on one side it overlooks the Cap d'Ail; on the other the Cap de Nice. For this setting, in which there are more rocks than shrubs, the two architects chose an architectonic structure in raw poured and reinforced concrete combined with dark-gray granite. These two basic materials underscore the noble austerity of an uncluttered architecture that is both contemporary and timeless. Rejecting factitious modernism and the lure of shifting fashion, Svetchine and Méchiche's design makes use of an enduring material that allows for a few compromises without in any way affecting the house's principled purity.

Like unadorned yet sophisticated building blocks, the building's vertical and horizontal lines provide contrast while adhering to the contours of the rock. Rock itself actually invades the interior of the house, where it is proudly and powerfully displayed in the foyer of the salon like modern sculpture. Outside, the dynamic energy of the rock is tempered by the geometric shape of the mirror-swimming pool and garden plots filled with sculptural tropical plants. Floor-to-ceiling glass walls erase the borderline between house and garden. A subtle and continuous dialogue modulated by sunlight and shade flows between interior and exterior, serving as the backdrop for a fabulous collection of art works installed in garden, bedrooms, and salons. A video by Bill Viola and photographs by Nan Goldin are combined with a sculpture by Anish Kapoor and paintings by Jean-Michel Basquiat. An installation by Piero Manzoni coexists with a sinuous red work by Mark Quinn.

The terraces, like the
house, serve as backdrops
for a magnificent
collection of contemporary
art featuring some of
the greatest painters
and sculptors of our era.
An abstract sculpture
by Sophia Vari faces
a yellow, rounded
installation by Gary
Young (left). The
swimming pool, which
follows the jagged
contour of the rocks, is
divided into several
interconnecting geometric
sections (above).

To the right of the nail-studded main entrance door, a monumental bronze bas-relief by Botero depicts a pair of mythic lovers shown from the back—a tribute to the master and mistress of the house (left, top). Inside and outside the house, molded reinforced concrete, with its inherent natural rawness and elegance, harmonizes with the local rock (right). In the living area, an illuminated metal composition by Lucio Fontana echoes the untamed nature that invades the foyer (left, bottom).

Frédéric Méchiche was inspired by the strict lines of the house's architecture when he produced his designs for the garden furniture—he created rectangular black metal chairs and tables that represent perfectly functional geometric solutions. Visitors will nevertheless note a contrast between the open-plan reception rooms and the cozy serenity of the wing that is reserved for the masters of the house. There, the bedroom and the living area, paneled in blond wood, project a hushed intimacy that features soft colors and sensuously luxurious materials. Heavy cashmere curtains open at the flick of a finger onto a landscape of shrubbery and rocks etched against the blue sea.

"The decor," explains Frédéric Méchiche, "reflects the owners' lifestyle. This villa is designed like a novel. I observed and questioned my clients, who soon became friends, about the way they live on the Côte d'Azur. From the first glass of orange juice at breakfast until the last nightcap, from morning shower to evening bath, frugal lunch to brilliant reception, I analyzed every activity in order to create the appropriate setting, lit in an appropriate way."

Functionality and ergonomics are key elements of the specifications that the two architects worked from, but neither was allowed to interfere with esthetic considerations. A home is a lot more than an art gallery, even when art looms especially large in the life of the home's occupants. "Art mustn't be confused with decoration," Frédéric Méchiche reminds us. "A house is not a static space, it's a setting for everyday life. It can be uncomplicated, but it must be charged with the kind of emotion through which beauty, continuously redefined, marks every moment of the day and night."

The owners of this house had absolutely no reservations about using a combination of styles and objects from different civilizations and different eras. In the main salon, which has picture windows that open directly onto the exotic terrace garden outside, twentieth-century masterpieces stand next to a collection of pre-Colombian art (left, top). Above the table in the dining room, a red monochrome by Serge Poliakoff hangs next to a canvas by Andy Warhol (left, bottom). The suite assigned to the master of the house combines comfort, ease, and sensuality. In the bedroom, in harmony with panels of sanded oak, curtains enclose a sweet and gentle world. Two canvases by Keith Haring perform acrobatics over the bed (right, top). The elegant striped carpet on the bedroom floor is the work of Frédéric Méchiche (right, bottom).

On the upper floor,
a panel by Allan
McCollum entitled
Surrogates *explodes
with vivid shapes and
colors; these contrast
dramatically with the
immaculate white
of the area around it
(above). A Cistercian
mood of peaceful
spirituality reigns
in the main salon,
where furnishings by
architect Claudio
Silvestrin stand on a
floor that is paved, like
the rest of the house, in
Burgundy stone (right).*

A tribute to uncluttered space

"Luxury is space." This affirmation is proven irrefutably by Eva and Armand Bartos at their Provençal home in Le Muy, in the foothills of the Les Maures mountain range. These two art dealers and collectors have spent their summers in Provence for many years. Finally, thanks to friends who are also neighbors, they managed to purchase a property that comprised a large meadow and what seemed to be a disused barn. However, when they consulted the local archives, they learned that this building—now in ruins, but with foundations reaching deep into the earth—had been an inn for pilgrims making their way to Rome in the Middle Ages. The inn had originally been made up of two buildings, and was converted into a stable during the sixteenth century, at which time its arched medieval-style windows were plastered over.

"We didn't want to destroy the shape of original building," explains Armand Bartos. "So we commissioned the well-known contemporary architect Claudio Silvestrin to restore it. We'd seen a block of Victorian flats in which one unit had been restored by Silvestrin, and that clinched it for us. His work is a perfect example of Mies van der Rohe's theory—with which we agree—that "Less is more." We persuaded Silvestrin to accept the commission. He came, he saw, he designed the plans in a flash. We didn't have to say a thing…."

Visitors entering the house through the huge patinated wooden front door will stop in amazement on the threshold. The first thing that strikes the eye is the majesty of the design and the impression of emptiness. The room, as vast as the nave of a church, is lit by tall windows set into one wall. The sunlight enters obliquely, underscoring the spot's spirituality—its Cistercian mood.

Through the kitchen door at the far end of the room, another luminous beam of sunlight sculpts the space vertically. This turns the main room into a monumental geometric composition, like a piece of conceptual art. It could be an experimental reflection on art's essence. A little partition that Silvestrin decided to put up in the center of the room creates two separate salons, but in no way detracts from the spot's overall purity. One senses that the slightest note of color would be inappropriate, that traditional furniture would look awkward.

Viewed from the swimming pool, the house—formerly a barn—is devoid of ornament, apart from the windows and doors that pierce the façade like medieval sentry posts. The sole furnishings outside of the house are a rudimentary but imposing table, and a ledge that serves as a bench while also underscoring the structure's horizontal lines (above).

In the bathroom, which was wholly designed by Silvestrin, the oval tub and geometric form of the room create a perfect equilibrium (above). A minimalist staircase leads to the owners' private wing (right). The intimate bedroom suite is half-hidden behind a partition. The fireplace separates a little sitting room from the sleeping alcove, which is protected by mosquito netting (facing page).

Claudio Silvestrin designed most of the furniture himself. In one corner, a harmonious arrangement of coffee table, armchairs and two sofas (the latter upholstered in neutral colors or white) stands flush with the floor which, as in the rest of the house, is paved. The walls serve—of course—as a backdrop for monumental works of art. A monochrome installation in black wood by Alan Charlton, a painting by Peter Joseph, three Asmat shields and a ritual pirogue stand out against the white background. Next to the long refectory table in the kitchen, an installation by Maurizio Pellegrin adds a few touches of bright red to the wall, contrasting with a Chinese scroll depicting a wise man at the foot of a rocky cliff. This oriental composition's vertical lines echo those of the house itself, creating dynamic tension with the kitchen's horizontal counter.

A double sculpted staircase that splits in two halfway up takes visitors either to the master-bedroom or the guest-room wing. Here, there are more surprises in store. The spacious room under its huge white ceiling beams at first appears to be empty. On further investigation, however, an intimate space comes into view. Tucked behind a partition, it is organized around a fireplace framed by two windows. A bed shrouded in mosquito netting adds a romantic touch. "This is a nomad's bedroom," jokes Armand Bartos, referring to furnishings that are rudimentary compared with the architecture. A multicolored "object-demystifying" composition by Allan McCollum and a yellow-and-blue abstract painting by Tim Ebner hang on the walls. A forest of vertical terra-cotta posts—an installation by Xavier Wolski—rests on the floor.

The total absence of knickknacks and bibelots takes some getting used to. Objects, clothing, and books are concealed in cleverly designed storage areas. Doors spring open as if by magic to reveal a television set or a dressing table. Even the bathroom is uncluttered. Two windows overlooking the garden are artfully inserted into the bathroom wall above carved stone sinks. The view from these windows includes the famed rock of Roquebrune and its mistral-shattered summit. Directly below, safely sheltered behind a laurel hedge, a long swimming pool in perfect harmony with the spirit of the house runs along one wall. The shape of the pool displays a moving purity perfectly expressing the architect's goal of geometric perfection. This is no mere exercise in style and virtuosity, however; it's a house to live in, where one feels comfortable. A house in which people can concentrate on basics: the beauty and energy of life.

The house opens onto a
garden that has been left
semi-wild (above).
The living area is
reminiscent of a cruise
liner—a spiral staircase
with an Art Deco-style
banister leads to the
mezzanine, which is
designed like the gangway
on a ship. An austere
marquetry table holds a
collection of stone obelisks
and some art books (right).

Squaring stone in the Luberon

"All houses resemble the person who designed them," notes the owner of this stone residence hidden in a forest of evergreen oaks near Saint-Pantaléon, a hamlet not far from Gordes. This connoisseur of the fine arts wanted to create a generously proportioned contemporary building expressing a rational esthetic. For its design, he commissioned an Iranian architect—a woman named Nasrine Faghih, who is steeped in the culture of both East and West and widely respected for her elegant and understated work, along with two local architects, Pierre Croux and Michel Nembrini.

Nasrine designed the house's core, a spectacular living area that anchors the rest of the rooms. Built into a hillside that had to be excavated for the purpose, this luminous room is surrounded on three sides by a gallery on the floor above, off which the guest-rooms lead. The fourth side, punctuated by tall windows, faces a thickly wooded area in which nature has remained largely untamed.

Nasrine Faghih's impressive, rigorously elegant architectural style, influenced by Le Corbusier, makes majestic use of space. When the house's tall windows darken at nightfall, one might easily imagine oneself sailing away aboard an Art Deco cruise liner. This impression is reinforced by a climb up the nautical-style spiral staircase leading to the mezzanine. The land reasserts itself by day, however, in a vibrant symphony of green. To emphasize the interplay between indoors and out, Faghih used blond ash for floorboards and door frames.

Although there are few windows in the main façade, a connection with the outdoors is one of the owner's priorities. This is why he chose as a heat source a Scandinavian-style wood-burning stove rather than a traditional fireplace, which would have detracted and distracted from the view of sky and trees. For the installation of the wood-burner, he sought the advice of a friend, France Loeb, also an interior architect. Loeb, who understood the owner's sensibility, suggested placing leather-lined double doors on either side of the salon. Loeb also provided advice on the choice of furnishings, a methodical process carried out over several years. After weeks and months of searching, she located a work table in L'Isle-sur-la-Sorgue, and clean-lined chairs in Paris and Belgium. Contemporary paintings propped up on the floor, geometrical objects

The chimney of the Scandinavian stove is so slender that it does not block the view, so, during every season of the year, it is possible to enjoy the beauty of a garden that blends gradually into the forest of evergreen oaks beyond it. The owner uses the mezzanine to exhibit paintings, simply propping them up on the ash-wood floor (above).

The elegant ash-wood strips around the windows seem to frame the landscape outside like a painting (left, top). The clean geometric lines of the contemporary four-poster bed designed by Christian Liaigre, and covered with a spread by Edith Mézard, suits the master bedroom perfectly (left, bottom). The dining room, with its solid-oak table and chairs, reflects the same understated spirit as the rest of the house. An old painting portraying Saint Roch and his dog adds a warmly human touch to the room (right, above). Outside, a barely tamed garden evolves imperceptibly toward the edge of a wild forest. Framed by two plane trees, a row of tall French windows runs across the stone façade, which is edged with trimmed boxwood hedges. On the upper floor, on the far right, the guest-room is invaded by a luxuriant climbing wisteria (right).

and instruments, globes, obelisks, astrolabes, and armillary spheres simultaneously represent the apostles of knowledge and the echo of a cultural and philosophical message. Less, as Mies van der Rohe liked to say, is more….

The dining room and master bedroom also project a discreet understatement, which is perfectly integrated into the overall spirit of the house. A few pieces of furniture in fine wood—including a monumental wardrobe and a bed with an embossed coverlet—create a mood that is at the same time sensual and monastic. Each artfully placed object expresses an emotion, a preference, a memory.

A more recent addition, but in a style just as discreet, is the tower—half donjon, half dovecote—that rises up amid the trees. This small construction overlooking the larger and older one is a contrapuntal repetition—and mirror image—of the house's rectilinear architecture. Could this tower be the one component on the site most emblematic of its owner? We will never know. He, like his house, carefully protects his charm and his mystery.

A suite in minimalist white

Jacqueline Morabito has restored an old sheep barn in a spirit of strict minimalism, retaining only the building's basic structure. The white floor and walls underscore an airy structure traversed by a gangway (above). The simple fireplace, inserted into the center of a rectangular opening, provides warmth and color in the room. Two armchairs designed by Jacqueline face each other beyond an oversize sofa upholstered in linen (facing page).

In the middle of an olive grove near Saint-Paul-de-Vence, Jacqueline Morabito and her husband, architect Yves Bayard, have converted a sixteenth-century sheep barn into a house of great simplicity in which each component has a special significance. Sculptor, jewel-maker, designer, interior architect, and stylist, Jacqueline has multiple talents and responsibilities, dividing her time between projects that are both prestigious and demanding.

Jacqueline's garden faces the medieval village, and she cultivates it in both the literal and figural senses of the term. She left the rural landscape—divided into broad terraced fields—virtually unchanged, adding only a narrow swimming pool that could have served as a watering trough in the past century, as well as planting large clumps of mastic trees to soften the straight lines of the buildings. Their carefully tended beds are in harmony with the beautiful order of the olive grove that lies a few acres in the distance, and which still constitutes a thriving agricultural enterprise.

The terrain's linear geometry is echoed by the architectonic austerity of the large white house. A few steps lead down to the entrance of the house, which is protected by an old stone portico. A nineteenth-century wooden figure seated on a little iron bench immediately sets the tone: pure lines, beautiful materials, a sense of history and a touch of wit. Immediately, the omnipresence of white is striking: white for walls bare of decoration or paintings; white for the waxed concrete floor; white for upholstery and bed linens; and white, also, for the furniture itself and the lighting fixtures. "Non-color," accented by the elegant black triangle of a grand piano.

A sensation of weightlessness underlies this new approach to lifestyles. The horizontal lines of two fireplaces holding sculptural logs arranged by an artist's hand contrast with the impressive height of the ceiling, underscored by windows framed with unbleached-linen curtains. In the living area, oversize sofas are perfect for napping or reading, an architect's drafting table for serious work.

Tables, chairs, and stools displaying Jacqueline's creativity are taken from her designer collections in powdered-marble veneered wood or oxidized oak. Jacqueline Morabito is particularly interested in the hidden

From a ruined former sheepfold, Jacqueline Morabito and Yves Bayard have made a contemporary home that retains the rustic spirit of the property. The meticulously designed structure stands on a terrain of terraced fields, which are dotted with centuries-old trees. The property was once a working farm (above). Following the line of the terraces, and built at an angle to the main house, the swimming pool is edged with enormous mastic shrubs and overhung by olive trees (right).

nobility of functional objects: for example, the two zinc watering cans carefully arranged on the terrace might be an artist's installation. This appealing area is accented by an unusual touch—a Renaissance cabinet restored by Jacqueline.

Another baroque note is struck on the upper floor, in a collection of religious objects: a rosary, ex-voto images, a crucifix, a prie-dieu, a carved panel featuring two cherubs flying through the clouds. This inevitably raises the question: were these objects chosen for their contrasting esthetic properties, their form? Or for their spiritual significance, their substance? The answer is not that simple. Will the response be whispered by the architect Le Corbusier or the poet and screenwriter Jacques Prévert, whose black-and-white portraits have been placed casually on the floor? Is it to be found in one of the books lining a library reached by the airy suspended catwalk? Perhaps in André Gide's 1909 novel, *La Porte étroite*, a defense of fervor and discipline; or alternatively in the essay, *In Praise of Shadows*, by the Japanese novelist Tanizaki Junichiro, which explains the Japanese conception of beauty and casts doubt on the use of color. Or perhaps in Kasimir Malevich's monograph, with its freight of metaphysical speculation on the relationship of form to substance, on the quest for essentials and the perfect unity between matter and spirit. Truth, as cold and bare as in the beginning of time, hovers somewhere within this white house and under the olive trees outside.

The headboard of the bed next to a table topped with powdered marble is one of Jacqueline's finds—a piece of carved wood from a Greek monastery (right, top). The linen-draped windows open onto a terrace where Jacqueline exhibits her collection of watering cans. The room's austerity is tempered by a few touches evoking foreign lands: Turkish slippers; an old suitcase; neatly folded linens (above, left). In the bathroom, a basin stands on an oak table beside a mirror propped against the wall (right, bottom).

VILLAGE HOUSES

*U*nder the shade of a church steeple, huddled closely one against another, village houses today often provide refuges for artists and connoisseurs, who come to the region seeking a change of air. Within the intimacy of ancient stone walls, these houses transmit a legacy of traditional skills, and a respect for the beauty of craftsmanship. Depending on the taste of their owners, they might be restored in a spirit of authenticity; or, by contrast, given a resolutely contemporary treatment. Their secrets remain hidden behind wooden shutters weathered by the passage of time.

An architect's house with a view

The view of the church and rooftops of Saint-Paul-de-Vence, as seen from the terrace of Robert Dallas's house (preceding double page). The connecting kitchen-dining room, with its exposed wooden beams and shelves and its whitewashed walls, is a warm and welcoming spot. The unbleached-pine farmhouse table and armchairs harmonize with the simple, rustic decor.

The English have cultivated their love affair with the Côte d'Azur ever since the eighteenth century. A more recent convert to the area is Robert Dallas, who over thirty years ago fell in love with Saint-Paul-de-Vence and opened an architecture studio there. When it came time to build his dream house, he stayed right where he was, choosing a plot beyond the town ramparts that afforded an unobstructed view of the fortified village and the Mediterranean Sea—one of the loveliest sights along the coast. Nestled in greenery and protected by a centuries-old carob tree, Robert's home perfectly illustrates a philosophy based on the interplay between nature and architecture.

Dallas's own villa, like all the others he has built, reflects the lessons of the past. Whenever possible, he uses original materials (stone, tiles, window frames), rediscovering the traditions and craftsmanship of the past and adapting them to the demands of modern life.

The architect has created a dialogue between interior and exterior on the ground floor that has the effect of expanding the living space and springing surprises. For example, through the far windows of a series of living areas beginning at the solid-oak front door, the medieval village appears as if by magic above the trees bordering the lawn. The ground-floor rooms are paved with patinated red tiles and flooded with sunlight; this enters through sliding French doors that eliminate the boundary between house and garden. Paradoxically, Robert Dallas has created a sense of space through the use of traditional storage units (closets, cupboards, shelves) that are built into the walls. In the kitchen, open plaster shelves serve as a showcase for collections of colored glassware and personal souvenirs.

The sparsely furnished bedrooms open onto a terrace and a wrought-iron balcony overlooking the garden. The bedrooms project the same principles of simplicity, comfort, and well-being that are essential to Dallas and his wife Lone. "Architects should be forced to live in the houses they design," he claims. Robert Dallas is a master of dry British humor, but his clients are very serious—except when they gather on the covered terrace for a sizzling barbecue, one of his specialties. As gales of friendly laughter ring out, the village below sails through the moonlight like a stone ship on a dream sea.

The house's foyer leads to a paved courtyard, where the architecture studio is located. The entranceway irresistibly draws the eye to the view of the garden outside, thus linking interior and exterior (above). A highly functional headboard and set of shelves are built into the whitewashed wall. Exposed ceiling beams underscore the room's rustic quality (left).

The upper-floor terrace,
filled with climbing plants
and furnished like a
living room, affords a
view of hills and tiled
rooftops (above).
The salon above it is
heated by a stone fireplace
and contains Kees's and
Lilo's favorite furniture
and artworks. Shown here
is a large painting by
Francis Torrès (right).

A Renaissance house in Saint-Paul-de-Vence

At the heart of Saint-Paul-de-Vence, on a small village square in which a stone fountain cools the brows and hands of indefatigable tourists, a gallery of contemporary art hides discreetly behind a heavy wooden door. Lilo Marti, an alumna of the Bienne École des Arts Appliqués, has been defending her artistic convictions for almost fifteen years. When she first set eyes on this sixteenth-century house and the stunning view it affords of the valley below, she decided then and there to leave her native Switzerland and move in. Marti knew that restoring the centuries-old house would entail some challenges. The installation of modern plumbing and wiring required drilling through walls several feet thick and dealing with crooked surfaces devoid of right angles.

The ground floor of the house is used as an exhibition area. A spiral staircase adorned with a lion's head leads to the floors above. On the upper floor, a fine sunny room serving both as a dining room and as a gallery opens onto a ravishing terrace. With the arrival of spring, this is where Lilo and her husband Kees spend most of their time. Lilo chose clean-lined wrought-iron tables and chairs that echo the objets d'art around them: Indian lanterns, odd pieces of pottery acquired here and there, and painted tinware by Casadamont, an artist from the South of France. Exuberantly luxuriant wisteria and begonia framing the doors and windows add a touch of romantic intimacy to this summer salon A second and larger terrace above, filled with banana trees, forms a kind of oasis in the sunlight.

The living room next to the terrace displays the owners' passion for contemporary art and design. A table by Hannes Wettstein, a white-leather divan by Zanotta, a stool by Eileen Gray, and lighting fixtures by Ingo Maurer are perfectly at home among the works of art—sculptures and paintings by artists from throughout the world. The display also includes folk arts and crafts: wooden forms used by hatters and glove-makers stand next to earthenware oil jars and travel souvenirs. This stone house is a showcase in which past and present commingle and are mutually enhancing. "Art is a superlative form of life," says Lilo, who, though sometimes discouraged by fluctuations in the art market, is always eager to share her enthusiasms and her quest for beauty with others.

An old well in the corridor that leads out to the peaceful little village square serves as a bar during exhibition openings. On the Renaissance paved floor, an inset metal strip, a horizontal sculpture by Gouleven, and minimalist installations by Gerhard Doehler forge a link between past and present (above).

Frédéric Méchiche or "time regained" at Hyères

A spiral staircase leads to the little terrace (above). The walls of the salon are still covered with successive coats of paint, expertly applied over the centuries (facing page, top). A collection of wrought-iron objects and minimalist art works reflects Frédéric Méchiche's eclectic tastes (far right, top and center). The kitchen utensils are all in subtle shades of green (far right, bottom).

For Frédéric Méchiche, this little fisherman's cottage not far from the Mediterranean is an enchanted refuge where he can catch his breath and rediscover the simple, natural life. It is also a symbolic structure built on fantasies and literary allusions. As one of France's most renowned interior architects—responsible for the decoration of major luxury hotels and sublime villas and apartments on both sides of the Atlantic, and the creative force behind the interiors of numerous private planes and yachts—Méchiche is a man who believes in nourishing dreams.

"I found my house by chance," he explains. Located far from the coastline and the Moorish villas that made Hyères famous during the Gay Nineties, this little house stands near a fortified gate, at a bend in a lane running through the old city. It was in ruins, and had no running water.... But the keen eye of the master immediately discerned its great potential. Most importantly, the house had not been disfigured by the random addition of "modern conveniences." It still had its thick eighteenth-century painted walls and its original ceiling beams. But, best of all, it still retained its authentic elegance. "And of course," adds the house's owner, "with a central location like this, I can do my shopping on foot, pick out my own vegetables, and chat with the people in the market."

While preserving the hedonistic spirit of the eighteenth century, Frédéric Méchiche enlarged some of the rooms, modified doors and windows, and inverted the house's overall floor plan. On the upper floor is the master bedroom, where a wooden four-poster bed hung with a canopy of unbleached linen nestles inside an alcove. A Louis XV chair and a door with eighteenth-century paneling, fine as they are, play second-fiddle to the tiny window framing a vision that could have been painted by Matisse—palm-tree fronds, partially concealing the fourteenth-century church steeple, rise into an azure sky. The salon and kitchen installed beneath the rafters afford a magical view of the church and old city on one side, the indigo-blue sea on the other.

Although firmly rooted in the village, this house is definitely not deprived of the presence of nature. At the top of the house a little terrace nestles; it is covered in a profusion of plumbago, bougainvillea, jasmine, and wisteria that creep boldly into the dining room during the summer. Intimate starlit dinners among friends are unforgettable occasions.

Guests are bathed in the glow of candles and Moroccan lanterns with colored-glass shades as music rises from the town below; everyone is beguiled by the charm of a village house rich in history and the good life.

The furnishings in the salon have changed over the years, but its walls still display the blue tints of antique paint. The furniture today—Directoire armchairs, an early nineteenth-century wrought-iron table, and a few designs by Frédéric himself (such as the white sofa)—exhibit a shared affinity for clean-cut lines. This decorative scheme recently benefited from the addition of a discreet tribute to the designers of the 1940s and 1950s (tables by Saarinen, chairs by Bertoia) and other minimalists: rhythmic variations on the grid theme pioneered by Aurélie Nemours and François Morellet; or the linear, arcane mathematics of a few great Americans such as Donald Judd and Carl André.

With its emphasis on black-and-white, the harmony dear to Frédéric Méchiche is skillfully expressed through a combination of styles and periods. Understated elegance depends, in the twenty-first century—as it did in the eighteenth—on a subtle balance between substance and spirit.

A small window draped
in white opens onto a
plant-filled interior
courtyard (above).
The elegant living room,
with its black-and-white
checkerboard paved floor,
is a warm and refined
setting, featuring furniture
picked up at local
antique dealers'—an
original approach
practiced by this Italian
couple. Above the antique
mirror hangs a net dotted
with luminous balls,
designed by the master of
the house (right).

A theatrical setting on the ramparts of Ramatuelle

Since the beginning of the twentieth century, the little fishing villages on the coast of the Var, and the tiny hamlets in the back-country behind them, have been attracting writers, artists, celebrities, and socialites. One of the places that has seen its fair share of well-known inhabitants is the tiny hilltop village of Ramatuelle, with its narrow winding lanes and arched passageways, which stands on the Saint-Tropez peninsula. Above the village ramparts—erected as a defense against invading Saracens—is a small house once inhabited, successively, by the author Colette and the actor and director Orson Welles. Its next tenant, who for many years spent much of his private life there, was eternally youthful 1950s leading-man Gérard Philipe. First acclaimed by audiences for his role as the Prince of Hamburg, Philipe embodied a pure and romantic ideal—as does this house, which he loved. Philipe was buried in the Ramatuelle cemetery following his untimely death, and the town now holds an annual drama festival in his memory.

The house, today occupied by an Italian fashion model, is built on three levels. It opens directly onto a flower-filled terrace shaded by a canvas awning. This is connected to a kitchen-dining room which is lit, in cooler weather, by crackling flames in the fireplace. This room—dark and mysterious under its ocher ceiling—is an inviting spot for winter gatherings. Its exquisitely simple, subtly tinted white-and-beige color scheme and walls of hand-built stone are enchanting. A silex-toothed harrow hanging on the wall celebrates farm labor. The main furnishings are a garden table surrounded by a set of French park-chairs. Fabric—silks, Indian cottons, voile, lace tablecloths—softens the stone with its elegant folds. The little whitewashed bedroom at the rear of the house has an intimate appeal. A staircase designed by an American sculptor friend leads from the lower level of the house to the light-filled living room above, where a connecting terrace overlooks the old village of Ramatuelle. Antique black-and-white floor tiles add a note of elegance, while rustic furniture and objets d'art—ceramics, mirrors found in regional secondhand shops—pay tribute to a typically Provençal way of life.

The romantic bedroom next to the living room affords a view of the sea through its picture window. A small table draped in linen displays a brass candelabra and some African necklaces. A deconstructed white dress

Three chairs are placed around the Louis XV table, which has been covered with a lace tablecloth for breakfast. Near the wrought-iron table in the background, a bench built into the wall displays a collection of cushions covered in exotic silks.

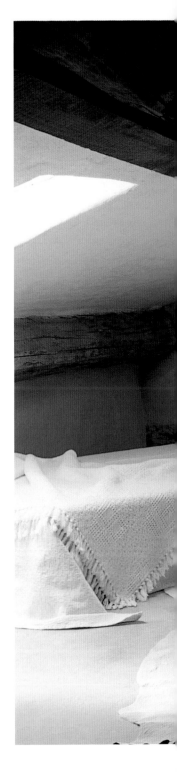

A rough whitewashed staircase built into the wall leads to a terrace overlooking the ramparts (far left, top). A small wrought-iron table with curved legs displays a collection of local crafts (left, top). The room below, which is darker, provides a much-appreciated refuge when a roaring fire warms the air in wintertime. Wire park-chairs surround a long table on which the mistress of the house has arranged a selection of ceramics (left, bottom). The alcove glimpsed through a door in the far wall serves as a guest-room. To the right, a little wooden staircase leads to the living room. The master bedroom under the rafters at the top of the house has a view of the sea. The same creamy white mood prevails on the top floor, where furniture and unusual accessories—like the wooden commode and the zebra skin—stand out against the uneven walls (right).

symbolizing the profession of the house's owner adds to the impression of purity and elegance projected by this refined room. The owner's husband, who shares her impeccable good taste, has embellished this summer retreat with a few works of his own—ingenious lighting fixtures that accent the decor's theatricality. Husband and wife are both fervent admirers of French culture, and both love the nooks and crannies of this house, dug into the rock almost like a cave. Nothing gives them more pleasure than holidays spent in a home that has kept all of its original charm, and all of its secrets.

Christian Tortu's village manor house

The master of the house wakes up to the sound of birdsong every morning.
His bedroom window opens onto the little garden, and benefits from a fine view
of the trees there. Antique furniture and curios picked up in Paris and throughout
the world combine to create a truly romantic setting.

Tucked away on a back street in Noves, a market town in the farming country near Avignon, is a house people tend not to notice as they go by. It belongs to designer Christian Tortu—florist to the stars, star of florists. Here, at the birthplace of Petrarch's muse, Laura, most of these passersby are more intent on shopping in the market than visiting the town's Sainte-Baudile church; similarly they might pass and repass in front of the great wooden door and closed shutters of this house without being aware of the wonderful story unfolding behind: the story of one man's fascination with the region.

Taking a break between numerous plane trips and a hundred exciting projects, this creative artist comes to Provence to restore his strength in the cool rooms of a manor house once owned by a provincial lawyer. "I was lucky to find a house that has remained unchanged for a century. I immediately fell in love with its design, its calm, and its spirit." The structure had been well maintained, and needed only a few repairs to the foundations. In the spacious foyer exhibiting the kind of ceremonial formality appropriate to a law practice, a stone staircase leads to the upper floor. Following an old Provençal tradition, Tortu places carafes of cool water for arriving guests on a sideboard by the door.

The dining-room walls display Züber scenic wallpaper, inviting guests to embark on exotic journeys. The somewhat faded tints of the paper have retained their poetic impact. Each panel illustrates scenes marked with charming detail and stunning perspectives. The long rustic table in the center of the room is perfect for every kind of entertaining. Silver candelabra with garlands of ivy and jasmine lend an additional poetic note that blends perfectly with china and glassware designed by Christian.

The relatively small kitchen is a meeting-place for friends who appreciate good food and wine. In fine weather, they move to the little courtyard transformed into a Mediterranean patio and filled with potted plants of all sizes. On an upper floor, the library has kept its original shelves and paintwork, a ravishing gray-blue enlivened with paintings by minor Provençal masters and an antique plaster cast representing the haughty profile of Laura de Noves—the great love of Petrarch's life, a woman he met in Avignon (on a bridge, of course), who was snatched away from him by untimely death. The table holds an old herbarium containing a

The French windows of this fine village manor house open onto an interior that Christian is in the process of restoring—when he has a moment between trips. He likes entertaining friends under the centuries-old plane tree, or simply resting in this peaceful spot (left). A still life composed by a master-hand: white orchids on a windowsill stand out against a background dominated by the leaves of the plane tree (above).

The upper-floor library has all the elegance typical of old manors, expressed through its antique floor tiles, eighteenth-century paneling with a faded gray-blue patina, and various objects purchased on impulse. A collection of treatises on botany, and books of poetry invite visitors to spend a moment of pleasurable browsing at the round table decorated with a bouquet of black arum lilies placed in a vase at its center (left).
The dining room, which immediately won Christian Tortu's heart, has retained its magnificent scenic wallpaper by Züber. Dinner guests feel as though they are embarking on a journey in very good company (right, top). People entering the house are greeted by a work chest decorated with small floral compositions that nestles under the wide baroque staircase with stone banisters (right, bottom).

selection of rare flowers (the latest experimentations of the house's owner), and objects designed by famous creative artists or picked up at secondhand shops from L'Isle-la-Sorgue to Seoul—all coexisting in friendly harmony.

The bedrooms, eclectically furnished, have lost nothing of their romantic spirit. The toile de Jouy covering walls and beds, the night-tables of uncertain provenance, the elegant bed linens and canopies—all reflect a philosophy of life based on wit, freedom, and a keen sense of beauty.

In the framework of a natural setting that is still striking and generous, each element of the house's decor contributes to the pleasure of being alive. As he puts the finishing touches on a huge bouquet of foliage gathered during a walk, Christian Tortu expounds his conviction that, "Enjoyment is fleeting and memory a thing of the moment." While we watch his sure hand at work and admire the final result, we are confident that—although what he says may indeed be true—paradise has not yet been lost.

MAS *AND* BASTIDES

*A*lthough mas, *(Provençal cottages),* *belong to a rural world where they blend into the landscape, bastides (farmhouses) dominate their surroundings. Whether simple or luxurious, these residences foster a lifestyle permeated with sweetness. In the Luberon and the foothills of the Alps, mas and bastides, restored with careful attention to detail by connoisseurs of old stone, offer their share of daily delight, and continue to provide the stuff from which dreams are made.*

Art on display at a bastide *near Aix*

Anduze urns and green shutters welcome visitors to the house (preceding double page).
In the foyer, an oversize sculpture keeps an eye on the staircase (above).
The dining room is filled with antique furniture and works of art (facing page).

P icture a *bastide* with straw-colored walls rising from a vineyard in the heart of the Aix region, which appropriates for its backdrop the distinctive silhouette of Mount Sainte-Victoire and the massive dome of Mount Olympe.

Visitors circling the small garden of boxwood and stepping onto the terrace shaded by plane trees are often tempted to invent a romantic past reaching back to the Age of Enlightenment for this Florentine-style palazzino. However, the house was actually built at the beginning of the twentieth century, in the Art Nouveau style—as proved by the sinuous frescoes that adorn the dovecote nearby. Under the eaves of its slightly overhanging roof, the large building's façade is accented by six green-shuttered windows in three rows. Harmony reigns outdoors, where a little stone fountain flanked by two cypress trees hardly disturbs the silence. A swimming pool lies below, framed by shrubbery concealed behind a screen of laurel.

But, push open the front door, and the tone abruptly changes! The first thing that greets the visitor's eye is a pretty room, furnished as an office and full of surprises. The furniture is traditional Provençal, but the works hanging on the walls are by the greatest of contemporary masters: Sol Lewitt, Thomas Hirschhorn, Francesco Clemente, Tony Cragg, Gerhard Richter, Guillermo Kuitca, Bertrand Lavier, Jenny Holzer, and Juan Uslé. This stunning collection reflects the avant-garde tastes of the mistress of the house, while a no less spectacular group of folk-art reflects that of its master.

Each room in the house serves as a setting for silent encounters between vividly primitive bestiaries from Latin America or the Orient, and works by today's foremost painters. And yet, these highly idiosyncratic collections harmonize perfectly with the decor around them. In the mostly red dining room, a large table draped with a cloth matching the printed cotton curtains at the windows holds a fruit stand as eye-catching as the photographs on the walls, by Nan Goldin among others. The same spirit of contradiction is repeated in the salon, where Biedermeier furnishings contrast with paintings by Willy Heeks and Jean-Charles Blais, and with a masterly screen by Jean-Michel Basquiat. On an old shop counter, retorts used to manufacture perfume and ceramic carafes face a bright-red

The kitchen, enlivened by bright yellow walls, beguiles the eye with a collection of folk art and still lifes (far left). In the living area, glass vases, ceramic carafes, and oversize model clay fruit, purchased at the Guadalajara market, stand on a draper's table. On the opposite wall, a disturbing portrait by Julio Galan stares down toward the stone fireplace (left). In the same room, behind a white sofa, an abstract photographic composition hangs over a Dutch marquetry desk. To the left, a lamp by Gae Aulenti lights up a triptych by Basquiat (right, above). In the corridor, the enigmatic subject of a large photograph in vivid colors contrasts with the Louis XV Provençal sideboard holding a curious mythical animal from Indonesia (far right). A backdrop for artworks, but above all "a house for living in," as the owner confirms.

studded fakir's heart by Cildo Meireles. All of this may startle visitors at first. However, in response to the house's charm, they quickly establish connections among the disparate artistic expressions offered to the eye.

The most spectacular sculpture, a huge female figure by Wang Du, poses provocatively at the foot of the stairs—and the upper floor is no less disconcerting. In the bedrooms and sunny yellow kitchen, the dialogue between primitive and folk art, between contemporary works and furniture picked up from antique dealers and secondhand shops in the area, continues. "Our house forms part of the Provençal landscape," notes the owner. "It still has its distinctive southern decorative style, slightly revised and modified—the perfect backdrop for our collections. But it's a house for living in, with children, dogs, the occasional argument, masses of flowers, and lots of pleasure...." It's also a magical setting for showing off the explosion of forms, materials, and media now occurring in the contemporary art world; and, simultaneously, for marking the disappearance of the frontiers separating art from life. Visitors touring the house cannot help but think of how lucky the young people invited here over the summer are to spend time in a place that's both so stimulating and so peaceful. Do they realize they're studying at the best of schools?

On leaving this lovely yellow manor house, one feels a tinge of regret, but also a newfound conviction that confrontations between disparate civilizations are not all that shocking; that, on the contrary, they broaden the horizons of eye and spirit. And so, one's final comment, uttered in a reverent whisper, is: "Bravo!"

An old mas *in the hills near Grasse*

Existing from time immemorial, dry-stone walls with built-in stairs follow the contour of the terraced garden at the foot of an old stone farmhouse, formerly the home of the British actor, Dirk Bogarde. Landscape architect Jacques Wirtz has redesigned the site, underscoring the geometry of the terrain and the structure of the house.

When the sky is swept clean by the mistral, you can see all the way to Corsica from the terrace of this old *mas* in the countryside behind Grasse. Set into a hill facing south, this house, sparkling in the sunshine above terraced olive groves and cypress trees, was once the home of British actor Dirk Bogarde. When Bogarde had a free moment between starring in films directed by some of the greatest figures of his time—Visconti, Resnais, Cavani, Losey—he would return to this country setting, and to the peace that contrasted so dramatically with the enigmatic and tormented roles he often played. The house is a former sheepfold that Bogarde converted without destroying its inherent charm. He added a kitchen, enlarged the terrace, reinforced retaining walls and terraced fields, and planted a vegetable garden. He spent his mornings in the privacy of a little room over the tool shed, where he penned autobiographical works and novels marked by a keen sensitivity to nature.

It is this calm, well-ordered, practical beauty that first attracted the house's present owners. They commissioned landscape architect Jacques Wirtz to redesign the ten-acre park, which retains the rural spirit of a countryside that for centuries past has borne traces of the human hand. Wirtz created new sight-lines in order to reframe the counterpoint of horizontal levels inscribed in the landscape, underscoring the rectangular swimming pool with an ivy border and a screen of oaks. He redesigned the frog pond first installed—and wittily described—by Bogarde, giving it a square shape perfectly adapted to the straight lines of the park.

The architecture of this *mas* harmonizes with the surrounding countryside, projecting the owners' taste for natural understatement and elegance. The house's façade, accented with windows framed by olive-leaf green shutters, has kept its purity of line and its rough, unfinished stonework. A friend and soul mate of the owners, Belgian antique dealer Axel Vervoordt, was a great help when it came time to furnish the interior. The building's structure has been altered slightly in order to make it more uniform. Bogarde's renovations were extended: the kitchen enlarged, and a superb stone wall—built according to traditional methods—added, to enclose the fourth side of an interior courtyard containing a flowering laurustinus bush.

The owners have sought
to recreate the original
spirit of this eighteenth-
century Provençal farm
house. The rustic little
dining room is furnished
with a simple wooden
table and chairs. There
are no paintings on
the walls, just a few
wickerwork objects,
which have been hung
alongside shutters
painted the color of olive
leaves (left). The
impressively thick walls
protect the farm from
inclement weather and
the mistral (above).

The entire house is a tribute to the classic craftsmanship of Provençal artisans. For the construction and renovation work, masons, carpenters, and blacksmiths used authentic materials and antique tools—thus exactly replicating the techniques of their ancestors.

On the ground floor and the floors above, the walls, beams, and ceilings in the foyer, office, and salons are whitewashed. The walls are bare, which is what the owners wanted. As they explain, "The views through windows opening onto a landscape that is sublime at every hour of the day are, for us, the most beautiful works of art one could wish for!"

The house's streamlined furnishings reflect a minimalist approach. Tables, chairs, ladders, and benches are carved from ordinary wood, mostly pine. Manufactured in northern Europe during the eighteenth and nineteenth centuries, and now worn smooth by time, all the pieces are admirable examples of ingenuity and elegance, perfectly combining form and function. The rooms in the house are not large, but without exception

The old kitchen with the original floor tiles is now a living area, heated by a large fireplace (facing page, top left). The bathrooms are built under the rafters (facing page, top right). The only painting in the house hangs from the wall of the master bedroom (facing page, bottom). On the terrace an elegant summer living room has been laid out under a trellis (left, top). In the center of an alley lined with olive trees is a swimming pool, perfectly integrated into its natural surroundings (left, bottom).

they exude the poetry found in old-fashioned interiors, and some—the dining room, for example—possess a calm harmony recalling paintings by Jean Baptiste Siméon Chardin.

Sunlight floods through the windows, casting shadows and glinting on an antique chest, a pebble-table by Axel Vervoordt, and some genuine collectors' items: enameled terra-cotta pieces and lamps made from willow-colored earthenware jars. A vivid symbol of hearth-and-home, the kitchen features daring touches of red and black: red for the antique Aubagne tiles covering the walls; black for the stove guarded by wooden candlesticks standing to attention like a row of mute sentinels. The windows of the monastically plain bedrooms with pitched ceilings open onto the surrounding countryside. A few colorful cushions accent the demure white coverlets on the beds. "We feel so at home here!" This spontaneous observation, endlessly repeated by the owners' guests, is also their favorite compliment.

Behind a garden chair
constructed from
driftwood, a border of
irises heralds a stretch of
farmland at the foot of
the Luberon (above).
France Loeb's large
kitchen is divided
into functional areas,
each with its own
visual focus (right).
On a bistro table with
wrought-iron legs
stands a collection of
nineteenth-century
terrines and apothecary
jars, surrounded by
crystal candlesticks.

An old farm in the Luberon

"Decoration comes from the heart," believes France Loeb, a talented interior designer who divides her time between Paris and the Luberon. Loeb's house—an old farm located in one of the prettiest villages on the south slope of the mountains—has been restored with patience and discernment. It perfectly expresses a professional philosophy based on careful thought and common sense. To this is added Loeb's innate sense of beauty and the urge to share her enthusiasms with a large family. She takes great pleasure in showing off photographs of this ancient farmhouse set in the midst of a vineyard and formerly occupied by the vintners themselves.

The grandeur of the Luberon countryside played a crucial role in the decision of France and her husband Michel to purchase the old building. When they moved in, their most pressing project was the garden. The majestic cedar overlooking the terrace is a reminder that their first task was to excavate the land around the house in order to free the rear side. Next, France designed a series of tiny garden "rooms"—bowers of greenery forming little corners of paradise. The entrance to the house is reached through two little paved courtyards in a geometric pattern shaded by blackberry bushes.

"We spend most of our time outdoors," notes France. "In general, we follow the shade." In the morning, the family breakfasts on an Italian baroque marble table next to the kitchen. This is the best spot for enjoying the wisteria blooms in springtime, followed by the cascades of antique roses that come into flower later, over the arbor. At noon, the family likes to gather for lunch around a table next to the fountain—after first sipping their aperitifs in a little interior courtyard separated from the rest of the garden by a stone arch covered with the huge cabbage roses that are prettily dubbed "nymphs' thighs." An ideal refuge during long, lazy afternoons is the terrace, which is shaded by palm trees. Accented here and there by Anduze vases, it affords a magical vision of this region in Provence, adding to the scene its little stone staircase that cuts vertically into the terraced garden, reveals a view of the vineyard, and seems to climb up and up, straight into the Luberon mountains.

The house's simply but elegantly arranged interior features an interplay of white, cream, and Nile green. The kitchen, with its vaulted

The master bedroom opens onto an outdoor salon that has been designed for refined, intimate living. Protected from the cold blast of the mistral, this little paved courtyard adjoins the kitchen and the dining room.

ceiling (common to all of the region's cellars), is a meeting-place for young and old. Boasting a light fixture picked up at a Paris flea market, a fireplace hand-built by a local artisan, and a butcher-block table, it admirably lends itself to impromptu meals and the gastronomic experiments of chefs of all ages. Next to the kitchen, furniture from the pantries and the outbuildings of the palace at Versailles reign with assumed modesty in a dining room with patinated walls that was once the farm's henhouse. Two large picture windows on either side of the room erase the boundary between house and garden, inviting the sunlight to sparkle on the teardrops of a sublime crystal chandelier within.

However, the salon is the room that most perfectly expresses the harmony and ease characterizing all of France Loeb's work. Comfortable sofas in white slip-covers welcome family and friends around a slatted-bamboo coffee table. The typically Provençal mantel over the fireplace holds small curiosities collected by the master of the house, Michel Loeb—a painter renowned for pointillist landscapes presenting a romantic and sometimes surreal vision of Provence.

"It's a house that breathes harmony, without impinging on individual creativity and spontaneity," remark close friends of France Loeb. "It's a house that brings everyone together," she replies—perhaps the finest compliment to a home-owner and hostess who is also an interior designer.

France Loeb has chosen a romantic ambience for this bedroom, in which antique curios bring back happy memories (left). The dining room, lit on both sides by French windows, is an elegant spot, in which every meal becomes a festive occasion. Antique-glass lamp chimneys arranged on a small table reflect the slightest glimmer of sunlight. Under the magnificent teardrop chandelier, the mistress of the house has expertly combined styles and materials—silver, crystal, wood, and china (right). A calm, natural, and refined harmony reigns in the living area, where well-stocked bookshelves prove a temptation for browsers (far right, top). The mantelpiece in the kitchen displays a collection of terra-cotta utensils. Wicker trays occupy the space traditionally filled by copper pots (far right, bottom).

A *little holiday* mas

In one of the rooms, baroque touches, such as a teardrop chandelier and gilded-wood framed mirror, temper the basic austerity of the setting (above). The kitchen adjoins a salon that has been furnished with a Napoleon III divan-bed (facing page). A zinc-topped table stands in front of the whitewashed-plaster fireplace (far right, top). Above the work counter, Bruno has cut a window in the wall, thus opening up the view onto the countryside (far right, bottom).

To provide an occasional escape from their life in academia, a couple in love with the Luberon realized a long-standing dream of theirs: to build a holiday home from the ruins of an old farmhouse. Not far from Cucuron, a peaceful little village on the southern slope of the Luberon, Michèle and Bruno Viard converted a decrepit eighteenth-century building into an intimate home featuring a decor that is elegant yet understated—minimalist, in fact. "We dreamt about this house for twenty years, and then, one day, we were able to buy it. It's a little miracle!" exclaim the lucky owners.

The Viards decided to plant olive groves rather than a real garden, and the same philosophy is evident in their restoration of the old farm. The couple took the beauty, harmony, and subtle contrasts of the building's original walls as their point of departure, a decision that has been amply vindicated. After long thought and much discussion, they eventually added a few rooms opening onto the stunning landscape outside.

As Bruno explains, "We chose a discreet, monochrome color scheme—shades of gray ranging from pale to charcoal—and, after stripping away every trace of varnish and wax, we decided to use the rawest of raw materials: cement, whitewash, unfinished wood, linen."

The rustic and poetic furnishings used in the house come from a secondhand shop in Marseilles, run by a friend specializing in old pieces glazed with the patina of time. Most of the walls are bare. Color is provided by flowers, vegetables from the market, and the clothes worn by the house's occupants. The bathrooms are spartan and (naturally) spacious. In a functional spirit borrowed from the Shakers that also highlights the purity and authenticity of original materials, stems from old glasses and stoppers from old carafes are used as wall pegs.

The life Bruno and Michèle Viard lead here during their holidays differs from their ordinary one, and is more profoundly connected with nature. Tables and chairs are shifted out of the sunlight and into the shade—placed among the olive trees at dawn and facing the sunset in the evening—so that each meal, depending on the time of day and the season, will also be a feast for the eye. Here, among grapevines and olive trees with silvery leaves rustling in the breeze, a return to authenticity can be savored deeply and in silence.

CABINS AND COTTAGES

*Y*ou don't have to be a psychoanalyst to interpret the "cabin dream." These rudimentary and precarious constructions, made of any old material, express a profound desire to reconnect both with nature, and with the magical world of childhood. Perched above a sea cove, the glorious Marseilles-style cabin celebrates the good life as lived on the Mediterranean coast. Built beside the water in the Camargue, isolated in the middle of a field, perched on an Aleppo pine or in the middle of a forest, cabins offer a lifestyle that is exhilarating, even when nourished by solitude and contemplation. These cabins and cottages in the heart of a still untamed Provence—these poetic refuges—are ultimate bastions of freedom.

A little cabin in the fields

In the open fields, between a linden tree and an olive grove, stands a cabin. The old irrigation basin has been converted into a swimming pool (preceding double page).
A ladder in the upper-floor bedroom leads to a loggia (above).
The ground-floor plan is ingenious. Cupboards are concealed behind shutters, a shower has been fitted into one corner of the kitchen. The sparsely furnished room remains cool even during the hottest weather (facing page).

Near the small sun-drenched village of Cucuron—a *castrum* founded by the Romans in the first century—a little cabin resembling a Nativity crèche stands outlined next to a vineyard. Probably once used to store tools or as a shepherd's refuge, it appealed to a pair of academics, Bruno and Michèle Viard, whose ruling passions are literature and interior decoration. This is just the kind of hill cabin extolled in the works of Jean Giono and Marcel Pagnol. Its rudimentary and bucolic aspects, blending perfectly into a setting of gray shutters and golden roof tiles, are the keys to its charm.

The cabin has an area of 125 square feet, providing just enough room for the couple to live comfortably. "Living well is my passion," remarks Michèle, who supervised every detail of the conversion work, changing the cabin's doors and windows to gain improved air circulation and comfort.

The surprisingly spacious vaulted ground-floor room is furnished with garden chairs and small antique pieces picked up at the flea market, or from a friend who runs a second-hand shop. Space is maximized by making every nook and cranny of the interior multifunctional. Also on the ground floor is the kitchen, used for preparing the delectable meals served on the upper-level terrace. Behind the kitchen is a shower stall, protected by a plain linen curtain hung from a bone-white wooden rod. The kitchen is also where baskets of fruit and vegetables from the market are stored. The work counter, like the floors, is made of cement—as smooth to the touch as to the eye—and reinforced with an iron rim.

The upper floor, opening onto a sunny terrace, contains just one bedroom. Friends staying in this guest room feel unusually comfortable there, enveloped in a warmth far from the world's struggles. A table set on the terrace in the shade of a linden tree is better than any of the region's restaurants. Inside, the wrought-iron bed with its white coverlet transforms nap-time into a sybaritic pleasure. In front of their little cabin, Michèle and Bruno have converted an old irrigation basin into an inviting swimming pool. The pool's supporting wall, wider at the base than at the top, affords a sensation of safety and strength. Swimming between the rows of grapevines in the vineyard is a delight, further enhanced by a view of the Luberon's voluptuous curves—as sensual as one of Matisse's models—against a horizon dominated by Le Mourre Nègre.

A treetop cabin

Inside this treetop cabin, a board can be lowered to make a bench for napping (far left, top). A fold-out desk has been installed under one of the windows, both of which have adjustable blinds (far left, bottom). From its perch in the branches of an Aleppo pine, the cabin affords a magical view of the landscape (facing page). The cabin is reached by a pathway cut between pines and evergreen oaks—allowing one to discover the Mediterranean forest's delights (right).

"I started building tree-houses when I was a boy…and when I retired from my career in advertising, I suddenly felt a yen to do it all over again," admits Alain Laurens, who hastens to add, "I was fascinated by Italo Calvino's book *The Baron in the Trees*. The hero, an eighteenth-century gentleman who climbed into a tree and never came down again, is a mythic hero. By rising above people and events, he was perceived as a champion of human rights and justice." The "cabin-in-the-treetops" dream reflects a deep-seated human desire to live in an intimate space at the heart of nature. This is not a regression, but an attempt to achieve detachment from life and from the self.

With the help of ingenious architect Daniel Dufour and skilled master carpenters and cabinet-makers, Alain Laurens set about building his tree-house of red cedar—a rot-resistant wood light enough in weight to be safely supported by the underlying frame—on the hills behind his house,

an old Provençal farmstead near Bonnieux that stands in the middle of an olive grove and is guarded by a hundred-year-old linden tree. Reactions were immediate: Laurens received a flood of orders from people who wanted exactly the same thing for themselves. So many commissions came in, he decided to form a company. All of which is perfectly understandable. It's an amazing experience to stand on a tree-house terrace some twenty feet above the ground and reach out to touch the branches of a 150-year-old Aleppo pine, to hear the rustling of leaves in the wind, to contemplate the valley of the Durance and the peak of Mount Lure with the Haute-Provence Alps in the distance, to fall peacefully asleep in a sky-top refuge scented with cedar and underbrush. Some of Laurens's friends come here to work, write, or—especially—to read. Others come to observe the herd of wild boar that thunders past every morning at the same time; still others to heal their stress and, who knows?, to find their roots, perhaps.

Le Corbusier's cabin

The little cabin's single room reflects the revolutionary theories of its designer. An early example of functional ergonomics, the room's every detail has been carefully thought out. A clinical sink juts from the wall under a cleverly constructed cupboard (above). In this meagre, austerely decorated space, the use of wood irresistibly recalls a ship's cabin (facing page). The furnishings consist solely of a table and stools made from crates (far right, top). A small window admits a slit of light over an adjustable chest (far right, bottom).

Beside the little Roquebrune railroad station, at the end of a path shimmering in light and shadow, stands a small log cabin overlooking a creek shaded by a carob tree. It's a basic "machine for living," designed by Charles-Édouard Jeanneret—Le Corbusier. His cabin is a goal for pilgrims and a shrine for meditation. Listed as a historic monument in 1996, the cabin is owned today by the commune of Roquebrune-Cap-Martin and the French Coastal Conservation Commission. It is open to the public on Tuesdays and Fridays.

It was Le Corbusier's first view of the sea from the heights of the acropolis in Athens that inspired his intense feeling for the beauty of the Parthenon, that majestic rectangular edifice exposed to the elements and emblematic of purity and rigor. After the trip to Greece, Le Corbusier developed a new and severely disciplined system of construction. This purist approach, rejecting ornamentation and camouflage, was reflected at an early date in a studio he designed for the painter Ozenfant (the Villa Savoye, with its roof-garden-solarium) and, thirty years later, in his "machines for living" project. He also began to think about building a cabin that would open onto an ideal landscape, mingling interior and exterior—a place where he could swim or sunbathe whenever he felt like it. While traveling through Roquebrune, he stopped off for a visit to Eileen Gray's house perched high above the Mediterranean. While there, he ate lunch every day at a small seaside restaurant named L'Étoile de Mer, owned by the Rebutato family, and recently willed to the French Coastal Conservation Commission. During the summer of 1951, struck anew by the beauty of this Homeric setting, Le Corbusier perched on the corner of a restaurant table, and in three-quarters of an hour sketched the plans for his cabin. It was to be a gift for his wife.

Le Corbusier's twelve-by-twelve-foot cabin is first and foremost a "machine for living," reduced to absolute essentials. Based on a square floor-plan, it's a space intended for work and leisure. Le Corbusier designed everything himself, down to the smallest detail; he also supervised the selection of furnishings and lighting. When he and his wife first occupied the cabin, in August 1952, he scrutinized its every component with a critical eye. Soon afterward, he added to his cabin a studio measuring about thirty square feet, resting it on a foundation of railroad ties.

This little pine-bark seaside cabin, where Le Corbusier spent August holidays when he was at the height of his career, is not so much testament to a great man as "the expression of thoughts generated in the mind of a benevolent savage at peace with nature" (far left, top). A fresco painted on the wall of the hallway separating the cabin from the former restaurant amazes visitors with its daring subject and vivid colors (far left, bottom). The single room, designed like a ship's cabin, is paneled with plywood. A mirror fitted onto a window-shutter reflects the natural world without pulling it into the room (left). In this cramped space, the view of the Mediterranean emphasizes the architect's existential attitude in response to the immensity of nature. Le Corbusier's cabin is a minimalist habitat, custom-designed for a man with simple tastes and an authentic spirit (right).

The main building's only room, with its sunshine-yellow floor, is built of unfinished plywood. Designed like the cabin on a ship, it is divided into two parts. For daytime there is a table, two stools, a closet, and bookshelves. For nighttime, there are two beds separated by a coffee table and a washstand. Three hatches and two windows, with square panes of glass and a mirror attached to the inside shutter, frame sublime views of Monaco on its rock. The terrace outside is like a stage set, with the Mediterranean Sea as a backdrop, irresistibly drawing the eye. Le Corbusier was nevertheless able to tear his eyes away from the view long enough to decorate the interior of his cabin and the L'Étoile de Mer restaurant next-door in his favorite colors—blue, red, yellow, green, and white. On the walls of the alley separating the cabin from the restaurant (today privately owned), he immediately painted a large phallic fresco. In his continuous quest for fresh architectural ideas, Le Corbusier combined wood with metal and invented a host of ingenious gadgets, such as the folding table with a mast for its pedestal, the latchet bedside table, the combination cabinet-stools, and the ingenious hanging and storage systems. At every step they take, visitors to the cabin will keenly sense the joy and vital energy of its designer.

Le Corbusier's almost revolutionary concept of space enabled him to develop a unique prosody of habitat, the "machine for living." This little log cabin represents the quintessential open, minimalist structure, drawing on a sense of space while at the same time reflecting a chosen lifestyle that renews the bonds between human beings and nature and emphasizes efficient function. As the vehicle for a novel ethic based on harmonious balance, Le Corbusier's cabin will remain, for future generations, the dazzling projection of a visionary and great reformer.

In cool weather, Mireille's guests gather around the white-plaster fireplace that casts its warm glow over the main room of her gatekeeper's cabin (above). This driftwood sideboard (left) owes its existence to the creative imagination of Mireille Desana. In the rear of the house, Mireille has reserved for her own use a cozy little bedroom with a view of reeds and marshlands (right). A later addition to the cabin is this glass-enclosed terrace, which has been painted Yves-Klein blue (facing page).

A gatekeepers' cottage in the Camargue

Standing out on the banks of the Launes pond, at the gates of Saintes-Maries-de-la-Mer, is a little whitewashed house with a tiled roof, a glassed-in terrace, and bright blue walls. Directly in front of it, an eccentric driftwood summerhouse faces an arrangement of driftwood that resembles a teepee. This is designer Mireille Desana's property—a mythic spot inhabited by black bulls, red flamingoes, and semi-wild white horses—located near the Rhône delta, where fresh and salt water meet.

Until 1991, Mireille lived in Aix-en-Provence. "I had a very pleasant life there, but I wanted something else. Untamed nature, the scent of salt and iodine." And so, in quest of adventure, she abandoned "civilization" and moved to the Camargue, where she now occupies a low-roofed cabin, sturdily built to withstand the mistral's sudden gales.

Mireille, who has a fertile imagination and deft hands, has filled her house with an extraordinary collection of furniture—almost as curious as her monument of driftwood outside. "The wood dries out faster when it's propped up like that," she explains. Her furniture—baroquely twisted tables, benches, and chairs fixed together with slightly rusty antique nails—project an almost mystic beauty, and seem to plunge us back into the realm of childhood. Torn from the riverbanks by the water's swift current, these driftwood branches are a gift from nature that Desana collects and then transforms according to the inspiration of the moment. Pliant and skin-smooth beneath her fingers, this wood, which has been bleached by time and the waters of the Rhône, acquires the fresh sensuality of a material restored to life.

Mireille goes "treasure-hunting" every morning, following paths along the river once taken by shepherds and their flocks seeking new pastures. Sometimes she climbs into her *roubine* (a type of flat-bottomed boat) and sets off for adventure through the waters of swamp and marsh.

Her house is furnished with natural, poetic creations that are currently highly prized in the sophisticated world of interior decoration. Gothic-style shelves, a curtained four-poster bed whose occupants must surely dream exotic dreams, grand thrones fit for kings, coffee tables for little girls' tea parties, display-cases for holding the latest finds collected from the shore. As majestic outside as in—especially when lit by a fire in the

fireplace—Mireille Desana's designs reconcile us with nature and the outdoor life. Mireille herself breathes a joie de vivre that she communicates effortlessly to others. Her newly inaugurated table-d'hôtes meal service (for groups of at least eight) has been enthusiastically received by visitors who appreciate fine food and the house's warm and generous atmosphere. In her tiny kitchen, Mireille adroitly produces sardine fritters, delectable fish soups, ravioli stuffed with subtly spiced vegetables, and peerless stews. When fishermen friends bring her their catch of the colorful shellfish known as *tellinas,* she stirs the little creatures into a scrambled-egg mixture that gourmets can't stop raving about. Mireille serves these marvels on lovely Provençal pottery dishes, at tables set up in the summerhouse or behind the glass windows of her enclosed terrace.

Visitors gazing at a flock of migrating birds overhead or a galloping white horse on the sands will feel ready to remake the world, disconnect the telephone, and sink into the beauty of this magical universe, hidden among the reeds between land and sea.

HISTORIC HOMES

*B*uilt for posterity, the homes described on the following pages needed only the dedication of a man or woman willing and able to revive them. From the Luberon mountain range to the shores of the Mediterranean, each of these manors and villas presents a fascinating history lesson. Here are stately homes that offer visitors a journey into the past—as do the châteaux of Grignan, Ansouis, Barbetane, Sauvan, Roquebrune, Cagnes, and Napoule, which are also open to the public.

The château de Gignac, in the Apt region

The foyer, paved with unpolished tiles, evokes the history of the Château de Gignac with as much eloquence as the portraits of the distinguished personages who once lived here. Under a large mirror, an eighteenth-century Italian console, decorated with delicate carvings, stands at the foot of the broad main staircase, which has retained its original banister (preceding double page). A series of salons with intricate moldings reflects the timeless elegance of the château (above).

When we think of earth tones, the ocher found on painters' palettes comes to mind. But ocher is just one of the many earth tones found on the "road of color" winding through the Apt region, around Roussillon and Rustrel, in a grandiose landscape of flamboyantly colored peaks and cliffs known as the "Provençal Colorado." Not far from Rustrel stands the tiny village of Gignac, one of the oldest gems in the Luberon crown.

The Château de Gignac looms above the pink-tiled roofs of the village like an antique engraving. It might almost be one of those fairy-tale castles sheltering a sleeping beauty or a hidden treasure. The open staircase climbing from cellars to attic has not yet yielded the answers to all of the castle's enigmas. Neither have the vaulted storerooms next to the kitchen, which surely contain mysterious secrets.

Built on a foundation of rock, this eighteenth-century castle is a far cry from the pretty follies dedicated to pleasure that were erected during the same century. Gignac's architecture is rational, logical, solid. Its thick, high walls provide an effective defense against the mistral, the harsh cold of winter nights, and the burning heat of long summers. And yet, behind the castle's forbidding walls and huge entrance door, at the foot of a graceful staircase reflected in the dulled tin of an immense mercury mirror, visitors immediately find themselves surrounded by the refined elegance of the eighteenth century. From a portrait hanging above the mirror's gilded frame, Jean-Marc Nattier, Prince of Béarn—in formal dress, wearing a powdered wig—courteously greets these newcomers to his home. They then move on to the salon-library, its Carpaccio-red walls underscoring the splendor of the heavy brocade drapes at the windows.

"When we bought this estate," recounts owner Michelle Joubert, a Paris-based interior designer, "it was in ruins. We restored it from top to bottom. Due to the ravages of time and bad weather, we had a lot of nasty surprises in store, but also great joy and pleasure." Furnishing the castle's many rooms was no easy task. Joubert ransacked auction rooms, nearby second-hand stores, and the Paris flea market for the treasures she eventually acquired: armchairs, couches, and love-seats, pier tables on delicately curved legs, and wardrobes with carved moldings handed down from generation to generation—or sometimes just the wardrobe doors

Private concerts are held in the music room every summer. Two mandolins, a bandoneon, and a flute, stand on the seventeenth-century mantel next to a baby-grand piano, patiently awaiting the musicians. This room sums up the aristocratic Provençal elegance: an ability to combine opposites with confidence, such as the crystal chandelier and terra-cotta floor tiles (left). A chair upholstered in priceless fabric adds its own note of refinement (above).

and a few decorative bits and pieces. Michelle, who is strongly attached to the natural riches of the "Provençal Colorado," personally supervised the restoration and finishing of all the furniture. Carefully measuring out natural pigments by hand and adding them to a chalk base, she has managed to create delectably inventive color combinations, including raspberry and cream, hard blue and putty. The kitchen, containing a long refectory table and sinks carved from white-veined red marble, is one of the most inviting rooms in the house.

When visitors climb the main staircase, they will inevitably be reminded of the brilliant summer receptions held here in the past. The staircase's stone steps were once swept by the long silk skirts of aristocratic young ladies who danced and chatted in the upper-floor ballroom, occasionally slipping out onto the orange-flower-scented terrace to take the air. The castle's present owner has retained this gala atmosphere by framing the wide windows in red silk, creating an illusion of even greater space with large mirrors, and hanging Venetian teardrop chandeliers from the ceiling. The music and billiard rooms next door are still much appreciated by male guests.

After the ball, those aristocratic young ladies of yore retired to sleep in the castle's bedrooms. The yellow bedroom with its four-poster bed has preserved all the nostalgic elegance and grace of a romantic scene painted by Jean Honoré Fragonard. Antique panels from an old screen frame a bed covered in lemon-yellow silk and lace. The sunroom opening onto a little terrace overlooking the inside courtyard boasts a fireplace and, above it, a mirror decorated with bunches of grapes. The Italian bedroom still has its original wallpaper, but is now more comfortable than it once was. Bathrooms in a vivid and somewhat theatrical style have been installed on every floor. One bathroom has a marble sink in the shape of a seashell; another, a roomy bathtub with clawed feet; and, yet others, rows of antique pottery and bottles standing in rows on dressing tables, or a little fireplace built into the wall so that one can enjoy the sight of flickering flames as one soaks in the tub. At Gignac the life of luxury has lost none of its elegance. Private concerts are sometimes held in the music room, fabulous banquets prepared in the kitchen, dreams still dreamt under the park's stately trees. A typical day might end with a dip in the swimming pool. Even this novelty, built a few years ago, bears a curious resemblance to an eighteenth-century mirror-pool.

In this bedroom with a gun-metal blue door, a papier-mâché chandelier hangs from the ceiling beams (far left, top). The bathrooms boast antique tiles and quaint accessories, and—in this case—a large bathtub with clawed feet (far left, bottom). In the upper-floor entranceway, a gilded-bronze lantern illuminates the molded ceiling (facing page). The marble kitchen sinks are edged with terra-cotta tiles. Michelle Joubert gathers her family for wintertime breakfasts around this Louis XV table (above).

The château de Mille, a fortress in the vineyards

History is sometimes recounted more convincingly by old stones than by schoolbooks. The stones of an exceptional residence—located in the vicinity of Apt and surrounded by vineyards and forests of oak and pine—have a particularly interesting story to tell. This gem from feudal times was once the summer residence of the Avignon popes. The Château de Mille—one of the two oldest in the region (the other is the Château de Ansouis)—is legendary. It was first mentioned by the Avignon Archives in 1238. Bertrand de Got served as bishop of Bordeaux and then later, under the name Clément V, became the first Avignon pope; he chose this spot in 1309 as a summer residence where he could escape the stifling heat of his Avignon palace. This is the pope—a vassal of Philippe le Bel—who, at the Council of Vienna, disbanded the Order of Knights Templars.

His castle-fortress, erected on a rocky peak in the middle of a vineyard, remained cool during the worst of the summer's heat and offered an especially secure haven not too far from Avignon. Standing near the Julian Bridge, built by the Romans on the Domitian Way, the building passed into the hands of the bishops of Apt, and was subsequently acquired by a series of prominent Provençal families. At the beginning of the twentieth century the estate was purchased by the Reynauds, master potters in Apt and ancestors of the current owner, Conrad Pinatel.

The Château de Mille's name raises numerous questions: was it built at a thousand-league milestone and named after the Latin word for one thousand, *mille*? Or is its name derived from "*milles*," the battalions of military guards posted on the tower of the Calavon valley fortress? Visitors who climb to the top of the tower can see for themselves that it affords an unobstructed view of the entire valley and the 350 acres surrounding the property. Of this, fully one-third is planted in vineyards, carefully tended according to traditional methods and producing marvelous *Appellation Contrôlée* vintages.

Today the Château de Mille, still marked by the proud beauty characteristic of fortified castles, surely has some fabulous secrets to reveal. Although the south side owes much to the seventeenth century, the north side has preserved its feudal style and defenses: crenellated walls, machicolated gateways, loopholes.

The stone walls of the Château de Mille form an ideal background against which to sample one of the estate's vintage wines under the shade of a plane tree (facing page). In the interior courtyard, a stone staircase with very uneven steps, carved out of the rock, leads to the chapel and to a dovecote, which was given as a privilege and symbol of nobility during the Middle Ages (above).

The kitchen has retained all of its original charm. The owner has set the refectory table with antique dishes, and suspended a set of copper cookware on the wall (right and below).

Paved with red floor tiles, the living room fits neatly into a spacious and magnificently vaulted space. A collection of antique china and fine, highly waxed furniture—including a walnut double-sideboard and a Louis XIII armchair—share a home in which history has left numerous traces (right).

The only way to reach the donjon, which contains a little chapel and a dovecote (a fifteenth-century feudal privilege), is by way of a staircase carved from rock running up one side of an interior courtyard behind a stone porch with a crenellated fronton. In this austere stone universe, an unexpected note of color is provided by vivid impatiens blooms growing around a lion's-head fountain.

The interior of the castle has retained its fine vaulted rooms and wide stone fireplaces, in which game is still roasted on a spit. Conrad Pinatel has assembled an impressive collection of antique furnishings: period highboys, majestic wardrobes, and historic portraits surrounded by pieces of Moustiers faïence and the characteristic mottled earthenware of Apt. On a superb walnut table stands Pinatel's remarkable collection of sterling-silver wine goblets and "*demoiselles d'Avignon*"—graceful ceramic carafes transported to the papal city by the boatmen of the Rhône.

Visitors never tire of hearing their host tell stories about all the famous people who were once guests at the castle; another gripping saga involves Pinatel's struggle to regain the Côtes du Luberon (*Appellation d'Origine Contrôlée*) designation for his estate's wine.

Today Château de Mille wines are available commercially, and regularly awarded medals and prizes in French national agricultural competitions. In other words, the saga had a happy ending—one that appears even happier to guests sitting under the shade of a lofty plane tree on the castle's terrace and sipping a glass of the white wine in question, which has "an intense bouquet marked by the scent of spring flowers."

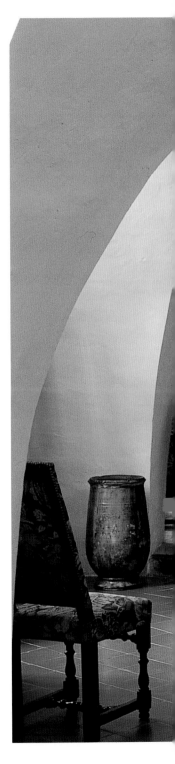

The swimming pool has been fashioned from a converted irrigation basin; from its dramatic position it overlooks the little tile-roofed village of Joucas and a multicolored mosaic of fields dotted with olive trees and greenery. Viewed from the upper terrace (above), the countryside unfolds in successive, perfectly ordered stages, extending from the twelfth-century fortress all the way to the blue slopes of the Luberon (right).

A book of hours for the Knights of Malta

High above Joucas, a little hilltop village overlooking a colorful patchwork of cultivated fields and clusters of trees, stands a fortified estate, witness to a past marked by the fervor and intolerance of the Wars of Religion. Today the home of internationally famed interior designer Dan Kiener, this fortress—like Notre-Dame de Sénanque—was built during the twelfth century. It was initially used as a headquarters by the commander of the Order of Hospitallers of Saint-John-of-Jerusalem, which changed its name to the Knights of Malta in 1530.

The Order's tradition of hospitality is generously maintained by the present owner, and the interiors of the buildings hidden behind the estate's stone walls have been decorated with an innate sense of beauty and drama. Perched like an eagle's nest on rocky crag, this former command-post affords a view composed, like an Italian fifteenth-century painting, of receding perspectives accented by the church towers rising from mountain villages, rows of cypress trees, orchards, olive groves, and fields of lavender.

The terraced gardens of the estate are filled with white flowers, and Dan Kiener's fortunate friends can contemplate a serene and peaceful Luberon from this impressive vantage point. The topmost terrace is shaded by the fronds of a weeping sophora tree, and made longer by an enclosed summer dining room, in which a strategically placed mirror reflects a magical view of the countryside below. It must be very difficult for visitors, who are no doubt hypnotized by the beauty of the site and the charm of their host, to believe that this outpost was a total ruin when Kiener first acquired it.

Using the building's overall form and harmonious proportions as his guide, Kiener's first tasks were to raze partitions in order to make the house habitable, and to equip the tower with a spiral staircase that he picked up from a local recyler. He then meticulously framed the windows so that each one would offer the sight of a living tableau or a view filled with poetry and enchantment.

For example, the view inscribed between two bronze sphinxes at one end of the main salon recalls paintings by René Magritte. The clean lines of the furnishings contrast unobtrusively with the fine art

This splendid spiral staircase was discovered at an architectural reclamation yard and was transported piece by piece to the entrance hallway of the fortress. Here, under the watchful eye of a Madonna, it curves up through the tower that leads to the master bedroom. Austere and imposing, the magnificent Renaissance wardrobe that stands opposite the door sets the tone for the whole place.

To emphasize the architecture and the purity of the decor, Dan Kiener designed a
half-canopy for his bed. He then draped it with floor-to-ceiling white linen
curtains to further emphasize the monastic spirit of this room, which is stone-paved.
Over the bed, a mirror framed in enamel is flanked by two exquisite
little Ingo Maurer lamps (above).

and architecture around them. The eye is drawn successively by a seventeenth-century Flemish tapestry, a broad-horned buffalo skull, a Renaissance sideboard, and a striking collection of hands carved from wood, bronze, and stone. Paintings and sketches illustrate one of Kiener's favorite themes: the staircase, which becomes a symbol of progress toward knowledge, of the ascension toward esoteric revelation. Dan Kiener is fascinated by symbolism in general and, specifically, by the symbolism he has managed to integrate into the decoration of his home and that leads to his own bedroom.

Here, two large windows face onto two different aspects of the landscape outside; bathed in the light that pours through them, the bedroom is soberly furnished with a four-poster bed. The bedside tables—antique pedestals from religious statuary—echo the extensive use of stone in the overall decorative scheme. The only elaborate pieces in this almost ascetic universe are a couch upholstered in gray tweed and designed by Kiener, a shell-framed mirror, and a collection of *intaglios*, which vividly accent the monastic white of a room paved in Oppedian stone. A born inventor, Dan Kiener has placed an ingenious sliding-mirror system over the windows by each bathroom sink, thus shielding these rooms from any prying glances.

As a tribute to the tradition of hospitality practiced by the Knights of Malta, Dan converted the little Romanesque chapel below the main house into a guest house. Drawing on an arc-and-circle theme, he installed a spectacular chandelier that can be raised or lowered by means of a pulley. Other additions—such as the mechanism from a church clock, a Renaissance cabinet, an elaborate round mirror from the 1930s, and paintings by old masters—create a surrealistic, bewitching, mystical, enigmatic atmosphere that is also prevalent in the rest of the house. The guest-house bathroom and green-carpeted bedroom cut from living rock are like mysterious grottoes.

The mood in the part of the house opening onto the interior courtyard is different: more intimate, imbued with more personal memories. This is where Dan retreats when the winter mistral rattles the solid-oak doors of the manor. It is here, in the privacy of his red bedroom, that he designs new stage settings; here that he defends, with the fervor of a knight in shining armor, the principles of a balance and measure serving harmony and beauty.

In the dining room, where a buffalo's head has been mounted under the curve of a walled and vaulted arch, a Renaissance sideboard keeps company with a round table; this is draped in white and surrounded by chairs with summery slip-covers (left). Lodged between linen curtains, in the embrasure of the window that has been cut into the thick walls, a comfortable banquette is covered with a scattering of cushions decorated with the Order of Malta cross (above).

A priory in the heart of the forest

In the interior courtyard, which has preserved its original austerity, stand two tables with wooden benches, tempering the harshness of the surrounding stone. The symbolic and evocative four-story tower of the Saint-Symphorien priory, which in past centuries was often used as a lookout post, is part of an old Romanesque convent built on this rocky promontory in the twelfth century (above).

As they reduce their speed on the winding road, people traveling by car between Buoux and Lourmarin never fail to notice a deliciously romantic vision by the wayside. Nestled in a grove of trees that curves around a bend stands a high stone tower with rows of paired arched windows and, like so many old houses in the region, a roof made up of flat paving stones. The sight inevitably recalls poems by Gérard de Nerval or fairy tales by Charles Perrault. The four-story tower, proudly exhibiting its symbolic and evocative power, forms part of an old Romanesque convent built on a rocky crag in the twelfth century. This spiritual landmark perched on its promontory overlooks a field of lavender with a small river, the Aiguebrun, running through it. A religious refuge visible from miles around, the Saint-Symphorien priory once played a strategic role: for many centuries, its bell tower was used as a lookout post. The priory attracted the attention of Prosper Mérimée during his stint as an Inspector—with extremely high standards—of Historic Monuments. However, it was not until the twentieth century that the priory finally earned its historic-monument listing.

The priory changed hands several times after the French Revolution. At one point it was owned by Roger Vadim, who lived there when he was married to Jane Fonda. The priory was subsequently purchased from Vadim by its present owner, Daniel Vial, who undertook the daunting task of restoration and reconstruction. The tower's impressive beauty was untouched by time, but the building below it was in ruins. A friend of Vial's, American interior designer Tony Ingrao, was commissioned to execute the restoration work.

Now, thanks to Ingrao, the building's rooms have recovered all of their original nobility. The monastic austerity of the original structure has been restored through the removal of modifications added over many years. The former chapel is now a salon lit by oblique sunbeams, as if by a projector. The vaulted stone ceiling is reinforced by a sturdy wooden framework. Below, on the chapel's large paving stones, stand comfortable armchairs and couches upholstered in white linen accented with black cushions. The minimalist approach is ideal for a setting punctuated by wrought-iron occasional pieces and heated by a vast open fireplace. This spectacular room extends into a small side-chapel with a mystical

*Viewed from the opposite
slope, the priory tower
dominates a luxuriant
setting in which a
swimming pool has been
built along the contours
of the rock (above).
The salons project a
monastic mood
appropriate to the spirit
of this retreat (left).*

Of modest proportions and remaining resolutely faithful to its past, the kitchen (right)—with its original fireplace and paving stones—has become the command center for dinners and receptions; these can be eaten outside under the shade of the evergreen oaks. The owner of the house often occupies the red bedroom, which has been decorated in a warm Provençal style (facing page, top). A path with stone steps takes visitors on a magical stroll around the priory (far right).

atmosphere. A collection of antique earthenware jars, a few pieces of peasant furniture, a bishop's chair, and a row of candles contribute to the overall mood of calm serenity. During the hot summer months, these two rooms are havens of coolness.

The kitchen, which is organized around a large eighteenth-century fireplace, is tucked between the large living area and an attractive guest room. Daniel Vial enjoys hosting elegant luncheons for his visitors, and it is in this kitchen that these meals are prepared, to be consumed under the shade of the evergreen oaks outside. When these convivial feasts come to an end, guests often head for the stone swimming pool, set into rock, providing bathers and sunbathers with an opportunity to contemplate the beauty of a landscape divided horizontally into blue strips of lavender all the way to the Aiguebrun valley.

Daniel Vial has reserved two rooms for his own use: one of them has red walls adorned with reproductions of drawings by Leonardo da Vinci; the other (of course) is in the tower. Might this mythical tower—which is the most difficult part of the estate to integrate into the overall pattern—express a leap toward spirituality, a desire for solitude and power? The owner, observing the rule of silence opposed on all monastic communities, answers only with a smile.

A pink palace on Saint-Jean-Cap-Ferrat

Flower beds filled with vibrantly colored blooms dot the lawns of this garden, which has been laid out in a formal French manner. Stone Medici urns and cherubim lend their grace to an enchanted realm (above).

Proudly dominating Cap Ferrat—a narrow wooded peninsula sheltering the fabulous homes of international celebrities and royalty—the Villa Ephrussi de Rothschild looms above the shores below. The Gulf of Eze lies to the east; the port of Villefranche to the west. Adjacent to the Villa des Cèdres (former fief of Belgian King Leopold II), the Château des Rochers (once home to Isadora Duncan), the Villa Santo Sospir ("tattooed" by Jean Cocteau), and the Villa Mauresque (Somerset Maugham's exotic refuge), is the villa-museum also known as "Ile-de-France," now owned by the Institut de France and open daily to the public.

The story of this villa would make a wonderfully dramatic play—one perfectly consistent with Jean Anouilh's stricture that plays should be pink, black, and brilliant. This play would be pink, for the color of the Venetian-style palazzino erected between 1905 and 1912 by Béatrice Ephrussi, née Rothschild, with the help of angelically patient Nice-born architect Aaron Messiah. And pink because—most importantly—pink was this poor little rich girl's favorite color. Black because, despite her assumed Marie-Antoinette style, the woman known as the "pink baroness" was never very happy in her villa, and occupied it for only a few months before taking off for luxurious anonymity on the transatlantic cruise liners she preferred. Black, too, for the tantrums staged by the baroness, who used to beat her gardeners in order to get her own way. Brilliant, because this villa exemplifies the uncurbed impulses of European plutocrats during a particular moment in time. Here we see the fads and fancies, the stubborn convictions, of an extravagant jazz-age lifestyle offering unlimited options to people whose sole goal in life was pleasure. This all-conquering nonconformism perfectly suited the personality of the baroness.

Today, the villa's salons continue to project the hothouse atmosphere of a patrician home, and contain remarkable collections of furniture, china, paintings, and objets d'art. In accordance with the baroness's wishes, the interior is unchanged; visitors still find themselves in the private home of a wealthy art lover. Louis XV and Louis XVI reception rooms—built around a Moorish-style patio, lined with marble columns—contain chairs, card tables, and pedestal tables by Hache and Riesener; ink-wash drawings by Fragonard; tapestries from Beauvais, Aubusson, and Gobelins; and treasures from the Far East. The most touching room of all is the

The upper-floor gallery, lined with wrought-iron openwork balustrades from Spain, overlooks the patio. The gallery is designed like the balcony in a theater, with the formal French garden starring on the stage below (left). From her terrace above the Bay of Villefranche, Béatrice Ephrussi dreamt of travel to exotic lands (above).

Salons and bedrooms display their splendor behind silken safety ropes. Beside the Venetian bed, a peignoir and a breakfast tray await the awakening of the baroness, who liked to pretend she was Marie-Antoinette (left, top). The clock on the exquisite Louis XVI dresser no longer counts the hours (left, bottom). In the boudoir adjoining the bedroom, an escritoire by Riesener, a silk-upholstered divan, and woodwork in the Pompeian style combine to create an atmosphere of refined elegance (right). In the Louis XV salon, armchairs upholstered in Beauvais needlepoint enhance the impact of the Aubusson tapestry on the wall (facing page, left). Detail of a late eighteenth-century painting on woodwork (facing page, center). The woodwork in the Louis XVI salon is from the Hôtel de Crillon. The Savonnerie tapestry once hung in the chapel at Versailles (facing page, right).

baroness's bedroom. Next to the bed covered with a silk spread—pink, of course—is a china tea service, an embroidered pleated negligée such as—who else?—Marie-Antoinette might have worn, embroidered mules, and a collection of somewhat faded old photographs. One of the photographs shows a proud, but melancholy, brunette beauty: Béatrice. Outside is a wrought-iron balcony, airy as lace, from which Béatrice could survey her garden, a seventeen-acre park owing its design to her stubborn willpower. The baroness's tantrums were legendary. Ferdinand Bac, who had heard about them, courageously refused a tempting offer to landscape the estate. Ultimately, the baroness succeeded in commissioning Achille Duchêne, a landscape architect famed on both sides of the Atlantic for gardens inspired by classical antiquity.

The fashion in gardens at the time strove for a kind of universalism. As at Les Colombières (the garden designed by Ferdinand Bac at Menton), the Villa Ephrussi gardens are planned in a succession of styles, unfolding like a journey around the world. Visitors pass from fountains bordered with papyrus to the pools in a fern-carpeted grotto; from the basins of the Spanish garden to a bit of Mexican desert; and from a precious-gem museum to a Florentine garden, a Japanese garden, a Provençal garden, and a stunning rose garden. Then, after climbing a steep path leading to the temple of love—a replica of the one at the Petit Trianon—they are next treated to the delightful view of a French-style garden containing a central water-lily pool reflecting the palazzino's pink façade. The Villa Ephrussi and its gardens can be rented for receptions or private concerts, and they have been used as a setting by numerous film directors, including Alfred Hitchcock for *To Catch A Thief* and Peter Ustinov for *Lady L.* Suspended high above the azure Mediterranean, they defy reason. The room overlooking the Villefranche Bay, once the baroness's Chinese salon, is now an elegant public restaurant/tearoom. It's a wonderful spot for lunch, an invitation to venture into the distant and poetic lands of dream and imagination. What does it matter if this hermetic world is nothing but an illusion? Its magic still casts a thrilling spell.

Théodore Reinach's dream of antiquity

Located on a rocky peninsula at Beaulieu-sur-Mer, the Villa Kérylos represents the materialization of a dream, the realization of a yearning, the outcome of a whim, and the fulfillment of a wish. A stone's throw away from Gustave Eiffel's holiday home, this enchanting site reminded Théodore Reinach—a wealthy archeologist, musicologist, stamp collector, and fervent Hellenist— of the Aegean Sea. Today the site is owned by the Institut de France, which has opened it to the public.

In common with several other eccentric millionaires of the 1920s, Reinach was obsessed with a bygone era. At La Napoule, Henry Clews dreamt of the Middle Ages. The golden age for Béatrice Ephrussi de Rothschild, the "pink baroness" whose villa is just across the way, was that happier time just before the French Revolution. Reinach's dream was of Periclean Greece, and he commissioned a young architect, Emmanuel Pontrémoli, to design a palace that would be the replica of an edifice of the fifth century B.C. He sank a huge fortune into the creation of a villa reflecting this ideal. Constructed around an atrium with an elegant peristyle, the imposing white building admits floods of bright Mediterranean sunlight through its large windows.

For the decoration of his palace, Reinach hired an entire team of scholar-artisans: Gasq, a specialist in moldings; Lenoble, charged with researching original glazing techniques for the tableware; Jaulmes and Karboswki for studying the thousands of documents and archives on which the period frescoes are based. Superb materials were used: tropical wood decorated with gold leaf, embroidered linens, sterling-silver mirrors, and extraordinary polychrome mosaics, patiently assembled by hand. Although the bronze-plated bathroom fixtures are glaringly modern, and electricity replaces oil in the alabaster lamps, the Carrara-marble thermal baths provide a suitably sybaritic setting for relaxing and chatting.

The library is dedicated to Athena and faces east, in order to protect from the sun the ancient and infinitely precious rolls of papyrus it contains. The furniture was designed by the great cabinet-maker Bettenfeld, who based his work on scenes from ancient Greek vases. Inlaid with ivory and mother-of-pearl, these pieces form part of a setting that is truly opulent. Guests invited to this imposing residence were given

With its marble panels, a portico supported by two Ionic columns, and an exquisite mosaic floor, the "Andron"—the room in a Greek house reserved exclusively for men— exhibits an elegance of peerless sophistication (left). The forecourts of the peristyle are decorated with frescoes illustrating the exploits of ancient Greek heroes (above).

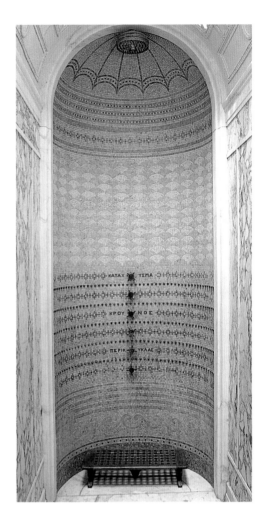

The shower, which has been constructed in the shape of an apse, is fed by rainwater, as it would have been in ancient Greece (above, left). The antique tub in the bathroom has sterling silver faucets. Walls and floors are decorated with bas-reliefs and mosaics, fitted together with as much precision as if they were precious gems (above, right).

a chiton or chlamys in the ancient Greek style to wear for dinner, at which they reclined on tricliniums while musicians plucked lyres and intoned *The Hymn to Apollo*, a musical score discovered at Delphi, transcribed by Reinach, and reworked by his friend Gabriel Fauré. The Pleyel company filled an unusual order for the villa's music room: an upright piano cleverly concealed behind marquetry panels. This dreamlike setting is decorated with a fabulous collection of amphorae, vases, lamps, statuettes, busts, and blown-glass fibulae.

Visitors wishing to prolong their enjoyment of this unique spot can pause for lunch in the ground-floor tearoom by the sea. As they contemplate the natural elements around them, while still under the spell of an esthetic based on harmony, order, and reason, they may begin to understand why the Villa Kérylos will, for all eternity, be known as Théodore Reinach's folly.

Blue predominates in Madame Reinach's bedroom, known as the Ornites and dedicated to Hera, goddess of the nuptial bed. The gold-leaf frescoes are decorated with peacock-feather patterns and winged figures more reminiscent of the Art Deco period than of Periclean Greece. A stool replicating those found in ancient Greek paintings stands beside a pale fluted column (left). The peristyle separating the house from the baths is supported by twelve Doric columns made from Carrara marble, and opens onto a central atrium planted with laurel, the tree associated with Apollo (right, above). Viewed from the beach at Beaulieu-sur-Mer, the white silhouette of the Villa Kérylos rises above the Baie des Fourmis. This exquisite spot reminded the fabulously wealthy Hellenist Théodore Reinach—who created the villa—of the Aegean Sea (right, bottom).

THE JOY OF COLLECTING

*C*onnoisseurs and collectors are always
amazed by the wealth of objects that fill
the world of antiques and crafts in Provence.
Numerous regional museums located in Arles,
Aix, Marseilles, Nice, and Grasse display the
genius of artists and artisans responsible for
the design of stunning objects and furnishings.
Tours of these museums provide an additional
source of knowledge, when visitors have the
chance to talk to specialists or other collectors
eager to share their passion. Thanks to these
enthusiasts, the Provençal heritage is more alive
today than ever before.

At Michel Biehn's house, fine embossed and silken fabrics vie with each other beneath an Art Deco screen (preceding double page). Jean-François Costa collects eighteenth-century travel cases. In this fitted Morocco leather case, each exquisite object has its own place (above). At Agnes Costa's, a quilted coverlet lies below a painting by M. Frydman (right). Silver clasps from a woman's cape displayed on a white embossed fabric (facing page).

THE RICHES OF PROVENCE

Over the centuries, Provence and the Mediterranean coast have acquired a unique and proud character that is rightly celebrated. The heritage of this sun-drenched southland, the fruit of traditions built up by the sweat of the brow—and sometimes the raised fist—is stunning in its richness and diversity. Because it manages to express a subtle balance between the aristocratic elegance of the eighteenth century and the cheerful simplicity of rural life, the Provençal style has been widely imitated and copied, and has truly stood the test of time.

The legend of Provence, which made its first appearance at the end of the luminous eighteenth century, is based on a spirit of independence and a taste for the pleasures of country life. Provence's golden age coincided with the Age of Enlightenment or, more precisely, with the three decades preceding the French Revolution. This period marked the emergence of a way of life that consisted of a rarely equaled homogeneity and refinement. Furnishings, fabrics, tableware, silverware, wrought iron, glass, mural decoration, and the visual arts all drew on the region's natural riches and the pragmatic and functional concerns of a cultivated and fully mature society. The decorative arts of the period reflected the same stylistic principles, while also borrowing a few charming and elegant details from an Orient more imagined than known.

Modern versions of authentic Provençal furnishings, fabrics, tableware, and even perfumes are as successful now as in the past, and numerous original masterpieces from the Provençal heritage are displayed by regional museums in Marseilles, Arles, Avignon, Nice, and Grasse. Some are also owned by individuals intent on preserving the region's glorious past and the memory of artisans and designers who have—through their skill and innate and polished sense of function and esthetics—made a significant contribution to the development of an authentic and autonomous Provençal decorative art form. Thanks to them, we are now discovering, as witnesses to a thriving culture, the different elements of a decor perfectly adapted to the spirit of its age, and to the demands of daily life, and devoted as much to utility as to beauty.

Gérard Guerre, an ardent connoisseur, collector, and antique dealer based in Avignon, was kind enough to open the doors of his home to us, sharing his love for and knowledge of Provençal furnishings, and paying hommage to the dexterity of the region's cabinet-makers and their tireless quest for pure, elegant forms. In L'Isle-sur-la-Sorgue, expert esthete and gourmet Michel Biehn likes nothing better than to display and explain a dazzling array of antique fabrics that, in their own way, illustrate the meeting between East and West. These hand-painted and print fabrics in cotton, linen, muslin, and silk—used for clothing and decoration—are embellished with embroidery and fancy stitching that reflect passing fashions or the seasons of the year. At Grasse, Agnès Costa—the daughter and talented representative of a family famed in the world of perfumery—took us on a tour of her family's two private museums and their home, initiating us into the secrets of a vocation practiced in the region ever since the sixteenth century. As visitors stroll among the copper retorts and glass perfume flasks, they learn how Grasse became a fragrance garden and the European capital of perfumery.

The following pages explain a way of life marked by wisdom, civility, subtlety, and harmony. A way of life that passes under our gaze like a lesson in history and sociology—vivid, fascinating, and rich in instruction.

Collections based on perfume

The doors to this town house, once owned by the Marquise Clapier-Cabris and now the Provençal Jewelry and Costume Museum, have retained their original patina. A carved and painted wooden Louis XV armchair upholstered in striped silk is draped with a quilted silk coverlet, also striped.

Perfume is often accorded the kind of reverence associated with religion. As the sentinel and reminder of past sensation, perfume returns again and again to haunt its devotees. François Costa, president and managing director of the Fragonard perfumery, has—through his professional activities—become a discriminating collector of objects connected with perfume. He and his wife Hélène have also, through their personal efforts, contributed to the renown of their city, Grasse, world capital of perfume. Thanks to their work, Grasse now boasts two private museums housing magnificent displays of Provençal craftsmanship.

The two museums are located on two narrow streets, and connected by a steep little staircase, in the old city, near the Princess Pauline Gardens with their stunning view of the city below, the Tanneron mountains, and the Mediterranean Sea. Although the flower market is still held under the arcades of the Place aux Aires, the inhabitants of Grasse no longer live solely for the seasonal bloom of local flowers, but now benefit from the perfume industry's expansion into the new field of food flavorings. The prestigious fragrance-production industry is still a thriving one, however. Recently launched Fragonard fragrance and toiletries lines, based on pure and natural ingredients, amply prove the success of new approaches to an old industry. Agnès and Françoise Costa, the worthy and responsible heirs of their parents Jean-François and Hélène, have enthusiastically taken up the torch passed on to them by the couple that originally held it so high.

Opened in 1978, in a town house once owned by the sisters' great-aunt, the Museum of Perfume retraces three thousand years of history through displays filling several floors of elegant and impeccably restored galleries. Visitors strolling through centuries of perfume manufacture will be fascinated by what they see: a collection of essence extractors, explanations of various distillation methods and the specific characteristics of the Grasse perfume industry, and rare and precious bergamot boxes once used for concealing love letters. The greatest periods of Provençal cabinet-making are also evoked in tasteful arrangements of eighteenth-century furniture: hope chests carved with symbols of love and marriage, walnut dressers with scrolled paneling, marquetry dressing tables in plain and Brazilian rosewood, and cane-backed chairs and armchairs with carved wooden frames. Paintings of elegant women at their dressing tables are echoed by sets of Moustiers faïence and—even more appropriately—by a collection of dressing cases that are genuine masterpieces.

As Agnès leafs through a weighty tome on the perfumer's art, she explains the history of her own company. "Fragonard has revamped its lines over the past few years, but has retained certain colors and codes. For example, the aluminum containers common in the industry, which we now gild in order to underscore the luxury of our product. Following our launch of the Soleil and Sorenza fragrances—a line of natural eaux de toilette for men and women—we are now planning household fragrances and a new product line, developed in cooperation with designer Jacqueline Morabito, which we'll add to the classic collections still selling very successfully in Fragonard boutiques."

Hélène Costa, who is fascinated by local history and folk costumes, is also a collector—in her case, of antique Provençal clothing and jewelry. At her home, and in the galleries of the Grasse Costume Museum, visitors will find displays featuring both the elegant clothing once worn by the lords and ladies of local manors, and the plainer attire of artisans and peasants. Petticoats, calicos, capes, scarves, *coiffes*, and aprons illustrate the life lived by local women through the seasons and the years. Quilted, embossed, and printed cottons, embroidered muslins, and delicate laces tell the story of their times. A collection of traditional jewelry evokes the degree of refinement achieved by the natives of Provence. The collection includes examples of the kind of pendant, decorated with a heart, hand, or flowers, that was traditionally presented by a mother-in-law to her son's bride—who would then hang the key to her new house and her embroidery scissors from it. Cape buckles in tooled or embossed silver and crucifixes set with more or less precious gems completed the basic set of jewelry for Provençal women. Here, as in the Fragonard boutiques, visitors can purchase reproductions of these original models, or pieces inspired by them but more modern in design.

This clothing and jewelry, tangibly symbolizing a regional culture and a living art—a reflection of the way people lived in the past—still inspire contemporary designers and connoisseurs, who are able to draw from the Provençal heritage an inexhaustible source of craftsmanship, color…and, perhaps, of joy.

The marble mantelpiece holds a collection of fragrance-essence retorts reflected in a mirror with an olive-leaf patterned frame. In the past these glass Florentine retorts and spouted vases were used for separating water from fragrance essences following distillation (left).

The carving on this wedding chest features musical instruments (above). Boxes made from bergamot bear witness to the dexterity of the local artisans, who molded the bark over a mandrel (left).

1

An interior designer's Oriental Provence

"What I'm interested in," explains Michel Biehn, a respected connoisseur and collector, "is the meeting between Provence and the Orient." At L'Isle-sur-la-Sorgue, in a large house that was once a draper's residence, he creates settings reflecting this encounter between East and West. Wedding chests swing open to reveal piles of quilted fabrics, each lovelier than the last; white embossed fabrics produced in the eighteenth and nineteenth centuries; and silk brocades woven in the Orient on hand looms.

"Thirty years ago," he reveals, "I purchased fabrics without knowing where they came from, without being able to put a date on them. At the time, fabric was the poor relation of the decorative arts, and this bothered me, so I started looking for information, scouring local archives, exploring the riches in private collections. The thing that struck me is that when weaving was mechanized, and the strands of yarn no longer passed between the thumb and index finger of a human hand, beauty vanished.… An irreparable rupture marked the end of fine craftsmanship."

Upstairs, our host accompanies us on a thrilling imaginary voyage. In one shuttered room stands a Chinese bed that might have come from the home of a wealthy opium smoker and that surely has exciting secrets to tell. The room next door contains an extraordinary bed designed by the great Viennese decorator, Josef Hoffmann, which Biehn has covered with a gold piqué fabric. The charm of Biehn's house can be explained, at least in part, by his taste for travel combined with an appreciation of sensuous materials and skilled craftsmanship, and by the importance he attributes to souvenirs with both sentimental and artistic value. "The combining of two distinct styles involves integrating elements that are foreign to one another," continues our historian, "but here, the encounter between two worlds reflects a basic affinity and, most importantly, a historic reality. Thanks to the keen commercial instincts of the Armenians, the coastal trading centers of the Levant—those towns located on the shores of countries ringing the Mediterranean—contributed to the growth of fruitful exchanges. Provence was the first region of France to discover fabrics from the Orient, and to adapt them for the development of a typically Provençal art."

Seeking increased prosperity, ingenious artisans plumbed the secrets of block printing, and reproduced the patterns of imported fabrics on local

At Michel Biehn's gallery-shop, antique embossed and quilted fabrics lie alongside Oriental silks (far left, top). A silk-upholstered Viennese bed is covered by a quilted Provençal spread (far left, bottom), while the medallions on a Chinese bed harmonize with a Louis XVI quilt (facing page). Exoticism invades the bathroom: pearly seashells are stacked on a small Chinese table against an Indian fabric at the window (left).

cotton. These *indiennes, siamoises, boucassins,* and *chafarcani* became highly fashionable in Paris and the provinces. Fabric pattern-designers, printers, and painters increased in number, despite a ban being placed on both the importation and production of Indian print and painted fabrics. The Provençal fabric industry flourished, adding the production of hand-crafted silks that were less lustrous but longer-wearing than the brocades and lampas silks woven in Lyon. The fad for imported Oriental fabrics—which were sometimes infested with vermin—was also responsible for the plague epidemic that decimated Provence in 1720.

Michel Biehn goes on with his story: "The fabric now considered a typically Provençal product would never have developed without a pre-existing pool of native skills. The amazing thing about those Provençal artisans was their ability to adapt and interpret the oriental influence in their own way." Which is why Biehn has devoted a lifetime to studying the marvels he collects, to perpetuating the skills responsible for them, and—most of all—to sharing his passion with others.

A great antique dealer in Avignon

When visitors cross the threshold of the Hôtel des Laurens in Avignon, what first strikes their gaze is this imposing balustraded main staircase and a superb Aubusson pastoral tapestry flanked by eighteenth-century gilded metal sconces.

Don't ever mention bread-boxes to Gérard Guerre! This dealer in antique furnishings and accessories occupies a magnificent town house, the Hôtel des Laurens, located on a small stone-paved square in the center of Avignon's old town. Bread-boxes, those virtually useless little perforated containers alien to any respectable Provençal stylistic canon, are anathema to him. Guerre explains the genesis of his expertise: "My interest in Provençal furniture first developed under the influence of two eminent dealers in the region, Vallat and Sérignon. It grew even stronger when I began furnishing my own house." But it is not just any house.

Guerre and his wife Françoise, both graduates of the Avignon École des Beaux-Arts, were fortunate enough to acquire the Hôtel des Laurens when they were very young. Since then, Gérard has worked continuously on the restoration of this noble structure, which was originally designed by the great seventeenth-century architect Frenici de La Valle. "The house is a listed historic monument and so, right from the start, I limited my collecting to pieces appropriate to the setting. This made me into a specialized generalist." Guerre keeps an open mind, but insists on compatibility among the objects he displays. The result is a lifestyle rather than a scholarly exercise. "I'm guided by emotion," he admits. "What I aim for is tranquil peace resigning harmoniously between two objects that are not necessarily from the same period."

His remark is borne out by a tour of the house. The majestic stone staircase is hung with a magnificent Aubusson tapestry. The painted ceiling is lit by a double-branched baroque lantern made from wrought iron and gilded lead. An immense gilt-framed mirror on the landing sums up the story of framing. Guerre is a specialist in the field of gilded wood—a luxury accessible only to a fortunate few—and has organized brilliant exhibitions around this theme. From him we learn that gilders and framers have worked together ever since the sixteenth century, often in cooperation with an art dealer. In Provence, the organization of separate craft guilds reflected the diverse skills involved in this intricate work, usually executed with sculptors' tools on soft ungrained linden wood. Gilding a single object—frame, mirror, looking-glass, barometer, console, pier glass—requires the combined talents of a preparer, a carver, a finisher, and a gilder.

A Virgin and Child at the foot of the staircase (left), carved friezes on the ceiling (below, top). Seventeenth- and eighteenth-century glassware: most of it comes from Trinquetaille (below, bottom).

Although provincial cabinet-makers have always copied Paris fashions, in Provence there is a difference: here there is systematic use of walnut wood. Gérard has lived among fine furnishings since earliest childhood, and his eye was quickly attracted by the beauty of walnut. Although he did not learn until later that furniture is designed to be made from a specific type of wood, and will be carved in order to take maximum advantage of that wood's capacity for reflecting light, he was early fascinated by the rituals connected with walnut. For example, on the birth of a girl, tradition decreed that her family cut down a walnut tree, season it, and then send it to the cabinet-maker to be transformed into a wedding chest for the girl's future marriage. On the ground floor of his house, under an imposing vaulted ceiling, Gérard Guerre today displays two superb pieces of walnut furniture: an eighteenth-century double wall cupboard designed for a farm in Haute Provence and decorated with a simple curved band running around the four straight panels, corners, and shelf; and a little late-seventeenth-century table made for a monk's cell at the Villeneuve-lès-Avignon monastery. The discreet nobility of these pieces is echoed by a group of glass jars and bottles from Trinquetaille, a factory that produced practical glass containers for truffles, olives, and wine.

"The only things I collect," says Gérard Guerre, "are items I need for the house, and also, at times, items with some regional historic significance. For example, the engraving based on paintings by Joseph Vernet, a seventeenth-century artist commissioned by the Comte de Marigny, the Marquise de Pompadour's brother, illustrating all the major ports of France." Here again, planning an exhibition afforded Gérard an opportunity to extend his expertise and share his enthusiasm with the public. For the last few years he has developed an interest in botany, a logical departure, as Provençal art draws its inspiration directly from nature.

"Life in Provence is affected more than elsewhere by the elements. People who want to cultivate a garden must have access to water and shade. They must also be humble and patient, and work one step at a time. The terraced fields characteristic of the Provençal landscape are built up slowly over the years. The 'good life' everybody talks about is based on hard labor. And yet, Provence is a hospitable land! It is this pride, these unremitting efforts than one does not talk about, that still moves me today"

WHERE TO STAY

Situated at the heart of a vineyard on the Bonnieux road, the Bastide de Marie is one of the most elegant guest houses in the Luberon (preceding double page). The bedrooms and both the private villas— rented by the week— all exude the simple yet refined spirit of Provence (above). Bought locally, engravings and a wooden sideboard decorate the dining room; its patinated walls and exposed beams harmonize perfectly with the few contemporary touches (right).

A NEW ART OF HOSPITALITY

People with no home of their own in Provence are lucky. No, really! Freed from constraint, they can, if they wish, set out each evening for new horizons—following the random meanderings of the road or a planned itinerary—and explore a region rife with charming hotels and guest houses, each more appealing than the last. These fortunate tourists can then return to their own homes, replete with the memory of experiences that will burnish the gray, overcast skies of other climes with azure and sunlight.

The hotels on the following pages were selected not for their fame or luxury, but for their atmosphere, their generous hospitality, and their way of expressing an authentic way of life—charming spots that display, in their respective styles, subtly different approaches to making guests feel at home. History is often part of the decor, tingeing each stay with romanticism and suspense. A Russian prince's castle and a 1930s hotel evocative of F. Scott Fitzgerald's Riviera, an old parish house, a cardinal's palace, and an elegant Provençal manor all invite guests to travel back in time, to live out their fantasies, and to savor a deliciously nostalgic aura of the past in a refined setting.

Guest houses like the Bastide de Marie in the Luberon are more intimate, secluded, and inviting—and have stories to tell that everyone will want to hear. On the Bonnieux road below Ménerbes, an abandoned seventeenth-century farmhouse converted into a country manor boasts several rustic buildings in which a lifestyle based on comfort, discreet luxury, and the natural beauty of the landscape is cultivated. Scattered throughout these sunny regions are quaint old farmhouses nestled in greenery—as well as attractively restored, more formal houses located at the center of villages—where nomads for a day or a weekend can enjoy the good life. People who are convinced they've seen and read everything, who are indifferent to the lure of easy living, almost certainly have yet to encounter—at Sivergues, atop a mountain peak in the Luberon—the rural and poetic retreat that transforms chance escapades into a festive occasion experienced outside of time.

Whether hotel or guest house, each spot described in the following pages has something very special to offer. All are listed in the "Useful Information" section at the back of the book. Planned like a map of the heart pointing south, here is a journey full of unexpected joys and delightful surprises.

The terraced swimming area, sheltered from the mistral by a wall of light-colored stone and a row of cypress trees, is composed of two interconnecting pools. In the heat of the day, this is a gathering spot for all of the house's guests. In the middle of the vineyard, two farm buildings converted into luxury private villas are available for weekly rental.

CHARMING HOTELS

*F*rom the Italian border to the Camargue, from the foothills of the Alps to the Luberon, on rocky mountain peaks or the shores of the Mediterranean, here is a selection of exceptional places to stay. Often the scene of historic events, today they welcome lovers of Provence and the Côte d'Azur in settings marked with exquisite taste and attention to detail. Whether in the luxury of a palace or château, the romantic setting of a manor or a farmhouse built on pilings over water, travelers can relive, in a contemporary version, the brilliant life once enjoyed in patrician dwellings or the thrills experienced by the last of the world's adventurers. A magical experience awaits.

Cardinal virtues in Avignon

La Mirande is a charming hotel located in the heart of Avignon just a few steps from the Palace of the Popes, and confirms the truth of the saying that piety and pleasure sometimes go together. This is a former cardinal's palace, which offers the Epicurean traveler a series of richly furnished and opulently decorated salons. Twenty comfortable, elegantly arranged bedrooms create an island of almost voluptuous beauty and calm—even when the Avignon drama festival is in full swing.

Guests studying their menus in the central atrium restaurant will not necessarily be reminded of the historic events that once occurred between these walls. In the seventeenth century the palace was converted into a private town house. Time passed, and three centuries later, in 1987, the Stein family acquired the stately home. They had the façade (attributed to Pierre Mignard, the seventeenth-century French painter and favorite of Louis XIV) remodeled by Avignon architect Gilles Grégoire. With the help of Parisian interior designer François-Joseph Graf, they used period materials to restore the building in its original seventeenth-century style.

It took three more years to restore the salons and bedrooms. Furnishings, doors, parquet floors, paintings, and mirrors are all period pieces that have been found through regional antique dealers. And yet, guests at La Mirande never feel as though they're stranded in a dusty museum. Those lucky enough to occupy one of the two rooms with a terrace will fully appreciate the spot's historic and hedonistic atmosphere, while also savoring the comfort of an extremely luxurious hotel.

The private salons and bedrooms at La Mirande evoke a dream of seventeenth-century opulence (preceding double page). Between the Louis XV salon papered in the "Chinoiserie" style (above) and the old kitchen (right, top), visitors embark on a journey through time and space.

This is also one of the rare places where guests can choose the era in which they would like to dine or enjoy a cup of tea. A medieval mood reigns over the decor of the vaulted cellars, one of which contains an original well. The Garden salon, which is in the style of Louis XV, succeeds in recalling, with its Venetian chandeliers, the graceful elegance of the eighteenth century, while the little Napoleon III dining room with its antique paneling creates a theatrical setting reminiscent of the Second Empire.

The grand principal dining room, which has walls hung with tapestries, closes once a week. This provides an excellent opportunity for guests to assemble in cheerful informality around a rustic table installed in the old nineteenth-century kitchen. It is wise to reserve your place for this event. One week per month (except in January, July, and August) prominent regional chefs conduct highly popular cooking classes in this room.

In Provençal, the word "*mirande*" means "marvelous." The hotel's name will seem perfectly apt to all those who have dined or spent the night in this extraordinary spot.

Slavic charm on the Riviera

Ollières and commissioned Polish architect Adam Dettloff, winner of the Prix de Rome, to enlarge and improve it. However, the couple had occupied the castle for only a few years when Madame Chevillot fell ill and died. Recalled to Moscow by the tsar, the prince sold his property, which subsequently passed through several hands before being purchased by its present owner, Robert Fontana, who has turned it into a hotel and restaurant of exceptional appeal.

The Château des Ollières has retained its turn-of-the-century Russian-accented style, its opulence, and its romantically nostalgic atmosphere. Painted ceilings illustrating scenes from antiquity, walls covered in silk or Venetian frappe velvet, huge mirrors adorned with plump cherubim, hand-painted paneling, antique furniture, paintings by old masters, and imitation-gothic stained-glass windows accent a lifestyle derived from the gleam of marble, gilding, and vividly colored silks.

Divided into small salons used as private dining rooms, the ground floor conceals a host of nooks and crannies. Dark wood paneling, damask brocade drapes, mahogany sideboards decorated with gilded bronze and holding crystal carafes—all pay tribute to the splendor of the French Second Empire. Comfortable, luxurious bedrooms in various styles are marked with a touch of Slavic eccentricity. Guests will feel themselves slipping into another time, participating in a fantasy reception presided over by the ghost of Prince Lobanov-Rostovsky, inconsolable widower. The Château des Ollières, a romantic spot par excellence, should be visited with curiosity and emotion...on tiptoe, so as not to disturb the slumber of a Sleeping Beauty still dreaming of her Prince Charming.

Well before the English arrived, the Russians were already influencing the history of the Côte d'Azur. They followed the example of Dowager Empress Alexandra Feodorovna, who always spent the winter season in Nice. By 1856 the Russians had established themselves in the city's Baumettes quarter. The Château des Ollières is located just a few steps away from the palace once belonging to Princess Elizabeth Vassilevna Kotschubey and now the city's Museum of Fine Arts. Flanked by rose trellises adorning the exact center of an exotic garden filled with rare plant species, Ollières was originally occupied by Prince Aleksey Lobanov-Rostovsky. "That place looks like an overturned armchair with its four feet in the air," French academician Louis Bertrand once slyly remarked as he strolled by.

While on a mission to Constantinople as minister of foreign affairs under Tsar Nicolas II, the prince fell in love with the French ambassador's wife, Madame Chevillot. He resigned his post and decided to move with his newfound love to Nice, where there was already a thriving community of patrician Russian expatriates. In 1885 he acquired the Château des

The neo-Gothic Château des Ollières is set among exotic gardens (left, top).

The flamboyant staircase leads to some luxurious bedrooms (above).

In the footsteps of Zelda on the Cap d'Antibes

People strolling through the pine woods on the Cap d'Antibes will inevitably be reminded of Scott Fitzgerald's heroes—men who crossed the Atlantic during the 1920s to display their blasé sophistication on the Riviera. Scott and Zelda stayed at the Hôtel Belles Rives, which at the time was a private villa near the home of their friends George and Sarah Murphy. This little palace resembling an ocean liner moored by the seaside is today one of the only hotels on the Côte d'Azur that has retained its original Art Deco spirit.

The extravagant presence of the legendary couple, touched by the scent of scandal, still hovers over the bar named after them. Next to the piano, one still finds fine early twentieth-century furniture, on a carpet designed by Sonia Delaunay. It doesn't take much imagination to picture Fitzgerald, playing at being Gatsby, listening to a Cole Porter tune while throwing back cocktail after cocktail—perhaps the "Blue Lagoons" that in the end make everything look blue.

The hotel's director, Casimir Estène, and its president, Estène's niece Marianne Estène-Chauvin, rejected the current fashion for new images confected by Parisian designers, deciding instead to retain their hotel's original identity and architecture. "A stay with us is like a cruise into the past for the span of an evening, a weekend, or a week," notes Marianne, who adds, "Guests can forget the world outside and live for the pleasure of the moment!"

Lunch is served by the seaside, at tables under parasols. In the evening, dinner at the La Passagère restaurant—with its 1930s decor and original gilded frescoes—is a delightful journey back in time. The red-and-blue tiled terrace overlooking the Mediterranean and filled with a riot of bougainvillea is the most romantic spot imaginable for a summertime tryst.

If you relish the atmosphere of long ocean cruises and exciting adventure stories, a visit to the Belles Rives is a must. The hotel has its own private dock and can be reached by sea. When arriving by boat, you proceed from the dock to an enchantingly retro elevator that will deliver you to your opulently decorated, air-conditioned room. Be sure to open your window wide every morning, and also late at night, when the stars come out over the bay. That is when, in the words of the French singer Charles Trenet, the sea sparkles with the silvery reflection of infinite beauty. Tender is the night!

Anchored like a ship in a bay on the Cap d'Antibes, the Belles Rives has preserved its Art Deco spirit (facing page). Dining on the terrace near a wall smothered in bougainvillea is one of the most delightful pleasures offered by the Côte d'Azur (far left, top and bottom). The dining room and bar combine the elegance of the 1920s with the charm of a seaside hotel (left and above).

Rooms over the water in the Camargue

If you're looking for something really different—and for fresh air, cool breezes, open space, and extraordinary fauna and flora—this is the place for you. Just outside of Arles, the two branches of the Rhône join to form an area that is half-land, half-water, and still relatively wild. This is the area known as the Camargue. Before you arrive at the legendary village of Saintes-Maries-de-la-Mer—a shrine for gypsy pilgrims who come here annually to honor their patron Saint Sarah—turn left, and prepare yourself for a few days of adventure outside ordinary time.

You've reached the recently opened, comfortable but unpretentious Mas des Arnelles, which extends a warm welcome to all nature lovers. Turning its back on the mistral, this hotel is constructed on pilings over the water. The building perfectly illustrates the successful integration of regional tradition and the contemporary spirit.

The architect drew his inspiration from local gatekeepers' cabins; these traditionally have roofs of tile laid over a base of reeds. The hotel's façade, reflected in a swimming pool that appears to vanish into the reeds, is edged with planks of unfinished wood painted an elegant pale gray and branded, like cattle, with the emblems of local herds. Rustic chairs and tables arranged around the pool invite you to enjoy a moment of rest, especially well deserved if you've been on one of those marvelous horseback-rides through the nearby marshes and rice paddies.

Each of the bedrooms that line the deck of the hotel is painted a different color; each of them also has an elegant adjoining bathroom. The Mas des Arnelles has its own restaurant, which serves a copious gourmet menu of savory Camargue specialties.

The hotel owns a fine stable of the snow-white horses for which the region is famous; you can be carried at a gallop along the riverbank, or at a sedate trot on the sandy paths winding between mirror-like ponds edged with clumps of reeds. In this breathtakingly beautiful landscape, black bulls, white horses, and pink flamingoes live peacefully together. The Camargue natives, riding by on their own horses, may not be able to express the emotions aroused by a panorama evoking the dawn of time, but even they will tell you that this is a place where you should inhale the salty, iodine scent of freedom as deeply as you can.

A headquarters for aficionados in Arles

The liveliest and most elegant square in Arles is the Place du Forum. Two Corinthian columns standing on a corner of the square are reminders that Arles was once a Roman colony, and also indicate the whereabouts of the Nord Pinus hotel. Even when not playing host to the Easter *féria*—festival—starring the best French and Spanish bullfighters, Arles—"a miniature Gallic Rome"—is the capital of French bullfighting, and the Nord Pinus hotel its temple.

This local institution's walls, like its guest book, are filled with souvenirs of the legendary era when bullfighter Miguel Domingúin was applauded by the likes of Pablo Picasso and Jean Cocteau. Crowned heads and headline-makers gathered for the corridas and the gala receptions given by two local celebrities of that earlier time, clown-acrobat Nello Bessières of the Médrano circus and his wife Germaine, a cabaret singer.

The Nord Pinus hotel sank into gradual decline after Nello and Germaine Bessières died, but is now being revived under the supervision of its new owner, Anne Igou. The hotel's soul—reflected in posters for historic corridas and celebrity photographs—has not been lost. Although the bar is no longer crowded with the colorful patrons of days gone by, a glance at the bullfighting icons and souvenirs lining its walls evokes ghostly voices from the past; but these are no longer heard among the clinking glasses.

The rustic, Arles-style furnishings in salons and bedrooms provide convincing proof of the skills possessed by local craftsmen. Accented by Peter Beard's photographs of the bush—a tribute to Ernest Hemingway—the decor is just as magical now as ever. Anne Igou has added

Venetian torches and teardrop chandeliers, and preserved the famous handrail that Germaine Bessières leaned on as she made her dramatic entrances down the hotel's main staircase.

Room Number 20 *(right)* was once reserved exclusively for visiting bullfighters, and is preserved as a museum-piece. On the mantelpiece stand the crucifix and statuettes of the Virgin that toreros prayed to before being taken to the arena. On their return, they stood on the balcony overlooking the Place du Forum and saluted the crowds of cheering fans in the street below. This room can be rented just like any other, and now allows animal-lovers and vegetarians an opportunity to become the new stars of the Nord Pinus hotel.

By Mount Ventoux, a table with a view

Visitors climbing up to the main square of the little fortified village of Crillon le Brave in the Comtat Venaissin area of Provence can admire the grapevines growing in disciplined rows at the foot of Mount Ventoux. From the terrace of the Hostellerie de Crillon le Brave they can also savor the pure air, peace, and beauty of a landscape redesigned by human hands. The man after whom the hotel is named, Crillon le Brave, was a local hero born in 1541 at Murs, who became a valiant captain and won the battle of Vervins for Henri IV. His family also gave its name to the famous Hôtel de Crillon in Paris. But by the early years of the twentieth century, this thriving hamlet, with a population of 800, was suffering from the lack of a reliable water supply; after the Second World War it fell into ruins and, following a severe drought, was virtually abandoned.

Today the name of Crillon le Brave, thanks to the beauty of its location and to the renown of the Hostellerie, has risen from the ashes to become a charming and lively village once more. The delightful Hostellerie de Crillon le Brave features a series of stone staircases linking the six village buildings it occupies: the presbytery and parish house, stables, the village school, a former silkworm house, and a sixteenth-century tower. Each of the hotel's thirty-one bedrooms is named for a local poet or celebrity, and decorated with fine furnishings and print fabrics in traditional Provençal style.

From the bedrooms, visitors can enjoy magical views of the hotel's Italian gardens and terraces, which face the slopes of Mount Ventoux, the peaks of Montmirail, and the tiled rooftops of the little Place de l'Église. Hotel guests particularly appreciate the swimming

The Hostellerie de Crillon le Brave offers the loveliest summer dining room that one can imagine. Tables are arranged on a balustraded terrace that commands a

spectacular view over the surrounding countryside (above). Salons and bedrooms perpetuate the timeless charm of Provence (right, top).

pool, a stone rectangle seamlessly integrated into the paving stones of the interior courtyards. People tend to linger over their alfresco luncheons, enjoying the peaceful gardens, admiring the rows of cypress trees encircling the fountain, and gazing dreamily at the vineyards below and the cherry orchards and olive groves in the distance.

After a tour of the village and a stop at the little chapel of Notre-Dame-des-Accès—built in 1720 as an offering to arrest the terrible famine then decimating Provence—you may well want to hurry back to the comfort of the Hostellerie, and the gourmet meals that await you there. Whether in the inviting atmosphere of the main dining room, or amid the more contemporary decor of the bistro, looking out to the interior courtyard, fine food is the keynote.

The charm of the surroundings and quality of the menu make the Hostellerie de Crillon le Brave a much sought-after spot for romantic evenings and the rare treat of an intimate dinner for two. Here is a place where the heritage of the past and the lifestyles of the present meet—an experience no one should miss.

An old family home

There are many different Provences: Paul Cézanne's Provence around Aix; novelist Jean Giono's Provence in the Manosque area; and director and playwright Marcel Pagnol's Provence, in and around Marseilles. Gémenos is in Pagnol country. Here, an old manor house once owned by the Marquis d'Albertas and now converted into a charming hotel might well have been the "*château de ma mère*" described by him. Located some twelve miles from Aix and Marseilles, near the coves of Cassis, this is a magical and impeccably run guest house.

The superb eighteenth-century façade of Le Relais is hidden behind groves of plane trees and an alley bordered by lindens. Glimmering in the sunlight filtered through the leaves of centuries-old trees, a stone cherub frolics with his dolphin in the centre of a pool edged with clumps of papyrus. Nothing could be more delightful than summer dinners under the plane trees. In the garden, guests will be entranced by the mellow, orderly landscape and the symphony of green contrasting with the arid slopes of the Sainte-Baume mountain range. Their appetite for further explorations of this historic setting will be whetted by what they see from the large hotel windows: glimpses of the lovely swimming pool on the left, and the tall arched glass panes of the orangery to the right.

The manor's original structure has been preserved. The red tiles used throughout the building lend a marvelous glow to the dining and reception rooms. In the largest of these, warmed by a wood fire crackling on the hearth, an Aubusson tapestry echoes the trees and in the garden. The more intimate library on the other side of the entrance door, its walls covered in toile de Jouy, is ideal for smaller gatherings.

Behind their solid wooden doors, the hotel's twenty-four bedrooms all contain tastefully arranged paintings and furniture: here a Renaissance cabinet; there a traditional wedding chest, Louis XV dresser, or canopied bed—all accented with ravishing fabrics. Each room is different; each has a working fireplace and a superb adjoining bathroom with marble sink. The entire house is imbued with the gracious refinement seen in a French Ancien-Régime painting. Gazing toward the end of the long garden, one might easily imagine witnessing the fêtes painted by Antoine Watteau, or see a group of masked players and dancers emerging in a swirl of whispered laughter from the evening shadows.

GUEST
HOUSES

*W*elcome havens of peace and
tranquility, these village houses
and country farms off the beaten track
are owned by people willing to share with
weary travelers an incomparable lifestyle,
expressed in different ways by different
individuals, against bucolic backdrops, at a
leisurely pace. Under the beamed ceiling of
a salon, in a garden arbor, or by the side of
a stone pool, life slips by. Simply. Calmly.

An old sheep farm in the Luberon

When you arrive in Sivergues, an isolated hamlet on the slopes of the Luberon, five miles from Bonnieux, you'll see a sign, next to the delightful Romanesque chapel of Saint-Trophime, announcing: "*Fin de la Route*," or "Road Ends Here." No, there's no mistake. Road or no road, this really is the way to Le Castelas, a former sheep barn built on the ruins of an old castle. Take a deep breath. The beauty of the landscape will take your breath away and you won't have much to spare now that you're standing at an altitude of 2,600 feet.

Clustered beside the rocks, these old fortified buildings—farmhouse, sheds, barns—have retained their nobly rustic appearance. The owner, a sturdy Sardinian goatherder named Gianni Ladu, who is as dark as his wife Ingrid is fair, likes to point out that, during the Middle Ages, Le Castelas was a favorite stop for pilgrims on their way to Santiago de Compostela. Without waiting to be asked, today's visitors inevitably launch into spontaneous praises of the grandiose panorama before them. The land between the sheep farm and the blue-tinted mountains in the distance is completely deserted—with the exception of a few children playing with the goats that are tethered in front of the house, or a shepherd crossing the plateau with his flock of sheep.

Despite its success, this remote guest house has lost none of its magic. Film stars, fashion models, famous writers, heads-of-state, royalty, hikers of every age and nationality, and a few knowledgeable tourists, all rub elbows around the dinner table presided over by Gianni. On soft summer nights these beautiful people gather on the terrace to admire the view; in wintertime they sit around a crackling open fire in the dining room. The menu features smoked country ham, salami of all sizes, spit-roasted kid, and an assortment of homemade cheeses, followed by marvelous desserts. All of which is accompanied, of course, by generous carafes of red or rosé wine.

Guests at Le Castelas socialize long into the evening, losing all sense of time as they sing and dance to the music of a guitar. Like everything else here, the bedrooms are unpretentious. Children usually prefer the dormitory. But everyone, without exception, has a single wish— to come back again next summer. It takes a good hour's hike up the lovely, fragrant mountainside to enjoy a well-earned rest at this timeless spot, although there is also a little parking lot just a few steps below the guest house—a godsend for non-athletes and car addicts. But what a shame!

A mas *near Saint-Rémy-de-Provence*

Fortunately, none of the original charm has been sacrificed to modernity. Here, there is no formal French garden with stiff patterns of boxwood—just an informal plot with comfortable chairs shaded by tall trees and, of course, a place to play pétanque. Guests gather for lunch inside the house, in small inviting rooms with exposed beams. Table decorations reflect the inspiration of the moment and the lucky finds of Albine, a passionate habitué of second-hand shops. The salon is painted gray and boasts a poetic floral decor: paintings of bouquets alternating with mirrors in gilded wooden frames.

Each of the fourteen bedrooms is unique; all are extremely romantic. One of them has lilac walls, lace curtains, and a fuchsia bathroom with an antique tub. Another expresses a Provençal atmosphere through a symphony of greens, a brick floor, and a large wrought-iron bed. Whether blue, ocher, or white, all the rooms reflect a lifestyle evoking family events and memories of the past.

On the edge of Eygalières, facing the Sainte-Sixte chapel—one of the loveliest in the region—stands the Mas dou Pastre, a delightful and somewhat nostalgic stop on the holiday road. Open for the past eleven years, this farmstead has retained all the charm of a family home, where the soul of Provence still sings its timeless song. The owners recount the history of their residence with pride and feeling. "Our ancestors were raised for generations in this building. They were shepherds from father to son, living here nine months of the year and spending the remaining three months in the Alpine meadows. In order to keep the farm in the family, we had to do something else with it, but we were determined to preserve its spirit and its decor."

When admiring the highly waxed antique furniture, carefully set dinner tables, walls decorated with herbaria, cross-stitch samplers, and somewhat faded photographs illustrating gala occasions of a bygone era, visitors feel as though they're being put in touch with a very recent past. These same visitors, after having refreshed themselves by swimming a few laps in the pool and before going in to a convivial dinner, might linger for a moment in the garden, beside the colorful caravans—which are actually ravishing and impeccably air-conditioned guest rooms arranged as though on a gypsy campsite—and dream, if only for a moment, of a different life.

A farm in the Alpine foothills

La Maison (also called Domaine de Bournissac) is a charming guest house located at Paluds-de-Noves, a step away from Saint-Rémy, and overlooking the Ventoux, the Alpine foothills, and the Luberon. It is difficult to imagine that this was once a farm whose output was reserved exclusively for supplying the summer residences of the bishops in the region.

Visitors crossing its threshold today are immediately attracted by the inviting atmosphere of the living areas, paved in stones that are inset with mosaic designs. Tastefully furnished in a Provençal style revised and updated by the mistress of the house, noted artist and interior designer Annie Zéau, these rooms provide a relaxed setting for every hour of the day: a reading nook with comfortable armchairs by the fireplace; another corner for enjoying an aperitif before dinner.

In the summer, guests need to plan their time. Those visitors seeking silence and calm will inevitably head for the terrace, which is shaded by a tall, centuries-old oak tree and affords a peaceful view of the surrounding countryside. Those preferring to sunbathe for a while, and afterward to take a refreshing swim, will stroll down to the pool. At noon, delicious light lunches are served in the seclusion of the walled patio. In the evening, dinner is served by candlelight—outdoors in the height of summer; under the ancient roof beams of the dining room in winter. The china and table linens designed by Annie Zéau in an elegant range of grays and beiges seem to stimulate the appetite.

It goes without saying that the talents of the mistress of the house are reflected in each of its thirteen bedrooms. Walls painted in antique colors, period furnishings, ravishing linen bedspreads and canopies produced by the owner's sister, and deliciously sophisticated bathrooms—all reflect the meticulous attention that is given to each detail. Visitors will certainly want to stay on for the night in the blue bedroom, or in the elegant and spacious suite with a raised alcove—or perhaps in the white bedroom, a romantic family duplex where children sleep soundly in twin beds under a pitched ceiling while the adults end the evening in front of the open stone fireplace below.

Everywhere, whether in the comfort of a bedroom or the elegance of a salon, guests will be charmed by this lovely Provençal home in which one feels so…at home!

A warm welcome for artists in Saignon

In Saignon, a fortified village on the north slope of the Luberon, contemporary-art lovers Kamilla Regent and Pierre Jaccaud found an old manor house, which they have converted into a guest house featuring rooms with a view. First as art collectors and then as directors of a gallery, Regent and Jaccaud wanted to settle in Provence while continuing to work with artists. This unusual inn welcomes paying guests for a very reasonable price, and offers accommodation free-of-charge to active painters and sculptors who can also display their works on the premises.

Pierre Jaccaud, the master of the house, explains his policy: "Because the art world is a sort of role playing that brings together both creators and purchasers, this place acts as an evolving stage on which these actors—or participants—can be 'presented' informally. As the seasons pass, the comings and goings of artists and collectors in itself generates a way of life right here."

The moment that the guests cross the threshold, they are confronted with a conceptual installation made of cloth partitions. Next to the kitchen—in which Kamilla simmers the jam made from fruit grown in the orchard—is the dining room, where guests gather for meals around a large refectory table. The living area serves as a general meeting place. During the evening, while taking care not to disturb the hazelwood mobile by Franck Morzuch *(above right)*, guests are able to linger over discussions of recent regional art exhibitions, or to listen to spontaneous recitals by visiting pianists.

Climbing up the stairs to the second floor, one enters an increasingly dreamlike world.

A Spoerri-style installation strewn over the floor reconstitutes the shattered fragments of an early-morning argument.

Each bedroom has its own personality. One is like a monastic cell. Next to it, a romantic boudoir with red walls *(facing page, top)* creates just the right atmosphere for sharing whispered secrets. The yellow bedroom contains an inviting antique wrought-iron bed.

The entire house is filled with objets d'art—enigmatic figures like the boy and his dog, by sculptor Andrzej Wrona *(facing page, left, bottom)*; ceramics from the 1950s; and, in front of a window, vividly colored crystal teardrops by Didier Tysseyre *(facing page, right, bottom)*. The eye roams from one thing to another, delighting in what it discovers. Under the trees in the enclosed garden *(facing page,*

center, bottom) is the summer dining room, reached by a bridge spanning a village lane. This is where Andrzej Wrona has installed another work, his circus figure, a young female bareback rider. While pondering this emblem of subjugator and subjugated, guests can sample fresh almonds as they await their aperitifs.

Outside and in, this haven for art offers a "dramaturgy of the intimate," in the words of Pierre, who adds, "Our home is a place where metamorphoses can occur. The works of art fill the space naturally and blend with their surroundings. We're like river-ferrymen. We bring together people who are interested in art and closely or remotely involved with it." The perspective at Saignon might seem slanted more toward the imaginary than the ordinary. It all depends on how you look at things.

A manor house in the Luberon

The charming Jas de Monsieur enjoys beautiful surroundings and has spacious and delightful bedrooms (above).

The Jas de Monsieur, located on the southern slope of the Luberon about seven miles from Grambois, has more than one story to tell. The land surrounding this fine manor house has a watering hole on it, and was once a hunting ground. A little later, a sheepfold and shelter for shepherds were erected on the spot. During the seventeenth century these were enlarged and improved, ultimately becoming a real manor house—as proved by the dovecote and the lure, an alley enclosed by overhanging trees used for trapping birds.

During the following century, the property was acquired by a Marseilles seed-merchant. Although he had a weakness for gambling, he nevertheless made elegant improvements to his new home. A fine foyer with a staircase separates the two salons, decorated with plaster moldings and formal fireplaces, that open onto the park. One salon served as a reception room, the other as a smoking room. The seed-merchant—the infamous "Monsieur" of the manor's title—was

an inveterate player of whist and backgammon, and he eventually lost his house at the gaming table. It then passed from hand to hand before being acquired some ten years ago by its current owners. "We were won over by this lovely building with an elegant stone façade that had not been disfigured by ill-conceived restoration work," they explain. Delighted to discover such period pieces as the kitchen's white-tiled, plaster-hooded "cook-stove," the paintings in the foyer, and the fireplaces with eighteenth-century lintels, they rolled up their sleeves and began converting their home into a guest house.

Canopy beds, oak wardrobes, and elegantly curved dressers furnish simple, spacious, and comfortable rooms, all with adjoining bath. A swimming pool resembling a natural pond offers relaxation to guests returning from hiking and cycling expeditions. Guests seeking a peaceful country setting often return for repeat visits, and are generous in their praise of the Jas de Monsieur and its authentic charm.

A refuge in the Aix countryside

Those looking for a place near Aix-en-Provence in which to spend a secluded weekend for two would be hard pressed to find a more romantic spot than La Pauline. Located in the Pinchinats area on the Sisteron road, this country inn, built during the French Directoire period, was the scene in 1807 of the beginning of a love affair between Napoleon Bonaparte's younger sister Pauline Borghèse and Comte Auguste de Forbin, dashing occupant of the neighboring Château Mignarde. The two met while taking the waters at Plombières. They fell in love, Pauline appointed him to the post of chamberlain, and they never parted again. The manor's current owners elaborate on the story, explaining that the vivacious and voluptuous Pauline once modeled for sculptor Antonio Canova, and that her brother Napoleon—then Emperor of France—was as jealous as any husband, keeping her under constant surveillance in an attempt to discourage her many suitors.

This bucolic retreat, which stands in a twenty-acre park, has been meticulously restored. The elegant decoration of the suite and four bedrooms in the little guest pavilion next to the main house echoes the graceful boxwood gardens. An old irrigation basin has been converted into a swimming pool. Below it, statues of Neptune and the huntress Diana, shaded by plane trees, are reflected in the waters of a stone pool dotted with water-lily blooms.

The almost imperial suite installed in the old orangery has red-tiled floors reflecting the color of its walls, and a view of the nearby olive grove. The four distinctive bedrooms are all spacious. Although recently built, they are eighteenth-century in spirit and vie in elegance with each other. Children of all ages will love the little gypsy caravan outside and its outrageously kitsch decor.

In an idyllic setting reviving the grace of a past era, La Pauline is an ideal refuge, where intimacy is combined with elegance.

Four bedrooms, one suite, and a caravan add their charm to that of the main house (left, top; above).

Statues dotting a poolside path (right, top) evoke a past era of unbridled pleasure-seeking.

A hilltop villa

Estelle Réale, a renowned interior designer responsible for some of the finest *bastide* conversions in the Alpine foothills, has turned an old inn—abandoned after its initial period of glorious splendor in the early twentieth century—into a quiet haven of peerless charm. The Villa Estelle, overlooked by the imposing Grimaldi château-museum, is nestled below the medieval village of Le-Haut-de-Cagnes. While respecting the spirit of a spot imbued with history, Réale has modernized the old building, which now accommodates guests in five comfortable bedrooms—each painted a different color, all elegantly furnished and air-conditioned.

Coddled by the discreetly attentive service, guests can breakfast on the terrace bordered with orange trees and laurels, or in the brick-walled dining room containing a long, family-style table. Before returning to their rooms at night, they may want to linger in front of the superb stone fireplace in Estelle's main salon for a chat, or to hear some of her thousand-and-one stories of the inn's glorious past.

Filmmaker Ingmar Bergman was a frequent guest, and wrote many of his justly celebrated screenplays while staying here. Royalty and celebrities—such as Orson Welles, Errol Flynn, Amedeo Modigliani, Chaim Soutine, and Jean Cocteau—habitually returned from masked balls, poetry readings, or exuberant candlelit dinners to end the evening with Suzy Solidor, an earlier occupant of the castle.

Today's guests, sinking into the cushions of the deep sofa next to a superb screen from the 1930s, can admire at leisure the present owner's taste, a harmonious and perfectly balanced blend of the classic and the Provençal, projected in their most refined and authentic form. The carpet and contemporary furnishings add a touch of modernity to this convivial room in which shades of beige and deep red create an intimate and inviting atmosphere.

Guests also have access to the kitchen, with its superb stove, and often feel more at home at Estelle's than they do in their own houses. The little stone-paved terrace a few steps down from the living room is a cool and peaceful spot from which to gaze at the stunning view of the valley below.

Estelle's private suite, exuding an aura of luxury and ease, is on the same level. Her bathroom boasts an imposing tub and decorative touches borrowed from the Far East. The sophisticated mirrors and tiger-pattern carpet combine elegance with a touch of whimsy. The linen-draped bedroom opens onto a sunny little terrace that resembles a romantic bower.

It's a point of honor with Estelle, who rises at dawn, to attend to each of her guests personally. She is keen that they should appreciate the charm of her home—and the voluptuous ease of this little town forgotten by time—as much as she does.

All the charm of a typical village dwelling is concentrated in the Villa Estelle salon and bedrooms (above, right). Early-morning sunlight warms the terrace decorated with orange trees and palms (above, left).

A family home in Lourmarin

At the foot of the castle in Lourmarin—a lovely village of which Albert Camus was extremely fond—the seventeenth-century house that was once a police station and then a coach inn now opens its doors to guests. Visitors are immediately taken by the charm of this spot, where the mistress of the premises extends a warm welcome to travelers. "My husband, an engineer at the École des Arts et Métiers and an interior decorator famous in Paris, Aix, and Marseilles, had a passion for restoring old houses and bringing them back to life," she reveals.

The courtyard that once resounded with the clatter of stagecoaches has been transformed into a garden, where a pair of centuries-old plane trees provide shade and cool breezes. Nearby, a hammock swings gently back and forth between two cypresses. Against a background of a burbling fountain, breakfast under the terrace trellis *(page 200)* is one of the most delightful moments of the day. The vaulted-stone ceiling of the ground floor has been stripped bare and the earthen floor paved with stone for the creation of an authentic and romantic room where guests can gather during the heat of the day. Used as a summer dining room or simply a cool resting-spot, it is adjoined by a large and efficient kitchen ideal for the preparation of elegant receptions.

The mistress of the house holds court on the upper floor, which is reached by way of an inside staircase or the little zinc-roofed turret. In these private quarters filled with objects and furnishings picked up at regional antique and second-hand shops, she likes to gather a few friends for a cup of tea and tell them the story behind a painting, an antique accessory, or a statue—like the seventeenth-century white-marble statue of Saint Christopher, or the wardrobe trunk once belonging to Maria Theresa of Austria that can be dismantled and laid flat for transport.

The upper floors of the house contain the five guest rooms. They, too, have benefited from meticulous attention: here we find a Louis Philippe escritoire in blond wood; a Venetian bedstead curtained in Braquenié fabric; or a nineteenth-century brass bed with copper knobs. Bedspreads and curtains echo the bouquets of fresh flowers. Each room has a small period fireplace. Guests love to light the logs on a cool evening and, in the glow of flickering flames, to study the objects around them, each one chosen with confident discernment. It is a setting reminiscent of a childhood home; one in which—with a little luck—time might stand still.

USEFUL INFORMATION

The listings below are not exhaustive, but have been carefully selected to include the people and places that demonstrate a quest for authenticity in their celebration of the charm and pleasure associated with living in Provence. Individual names and establishments are listed by region (French department) and by type, in order to underscore the various facets of life in the South of France. These listings reflect a collective research effort conducted by our qualified team of experts, and also include recommendations from informed contributors who live in Provence.

In this section, readers will be able to find contact information for the architects, landscape artists, and interior designers referred to in the preceding chapters. Those wishing to build, restore, furnish, or decorate a house; and those wishing to create a garden, can make use of this extensive selection of the best addresses in Provence and on the Côte d'Azur.

Museums and galleries are also included in our listings, though only those that deal exclusively with the traditional arts and lifestyles of Provence.

Readers will not be able to find the names of luxury hotels and trendy restaurants in this section. Instead, we have sought out charming little hotels and guest houses off the beaten path, where we hope our readers will enjoy memorable visits.

ARCHITECTS, INTERIOR DESIGNERS, AND DECORATORS

The dedicated men and women listed below are sensitive to the local terrain, to the environment, and to the architectural history of the region, defending a balanced and harmonious idea of beauty, in which geometry defines form.
Note: DPLG (diplomé par la gouvernement) is the accredited French degree in Architecture.

ALPES-MARITIMES

ANTONINO CASCIO
Les Hameaux du Soleil
06270 Villeneuve-Loubet
Tel.: +33 (0)4 92 02 91 11
(see pages 60, 68–71)
Cascio, a graduate of the Palermo School of Architecture, specializes in highly contemporary design. His villas, which combine concrete, wood, and glass, are spectacular without being ostentatious, and are always perfectly integrated into the site.

CABINET D'ARCHITECTURE ROBERT DALLAS
Quartier Sainte-Claire
06570 Saint-Paul
Tel.: +33 (0)4 93 32 55 55
(see pages 92–95)
Dubbed the architect of the stars, Robert Dallas builds and restores old Provençal farmhouses using recycled materials.

CHRISTOPHE PETITCOLLOT
551, chemin de Saint-Arnoux
Tourrettes-sur-Loup
Tel.: +33 (0)4 93 59 36 66
(see pages 60, 72–75)
Petitcollot, a DPLG architect, who holds teaching posts in the United States and Mexico, designs projects in a contemporary spirit, integrating different forms into a rigorous and coherent overall geometry.

LUC SVETCHINE
37, avenue Primrose
06000 Nice
Tel.: +33 (0)4 93 96 79 79
(see pages 76–79)
Svetchine is a DPLG architect who constructs, reconstructs, and restores luxury hotels and individual residences in a rigorous contemporary style in which pure geometry is emphasized.

BOUCHES-DU-RHÔNE

BUREAU D'ÉTUDES BRUNO LAFOURCADE
10, boulevard Mirabeau
13210 Saint-Rémy
Tel.: +33 (0)4 90 92 10 14
This talented self-made man specializes in the restoration of old farmhouses, carried out in an eighteenth-century spirit with meticulous attention to detail and a keen sense of elegance and balance.

PARIS REGION

NASRINE FAGHIH
72, rue de Turenne
75003 Paris
Tel.: +33 (0)1 48 04 96 65
(see pages 84–87)
Faghih, a DPLG architect who was born in Iran, treats tradition in new ways. She combines lessons learned from both East and West, while also adding touches derived from Le Corbusier, Philip Johnson, and Frank Lloyd Wright.

MICHELLE JOUBERT
81, rue de Lille
75007 Paris
Tel.: +33 (0)1 45 51 97 32
(see pages 138–141)
This interior designer works with character houses and apartments in Paris and the French provinces. Her display cabinets and bookcases eloquently express the timeless charm of her restorations, which are subtle and poetic.

BOUCHES-DU-RHÔNE

FRÉDÉRIC MÉCHICHE
4, rue de Thorigny
75003 Paris
Tel.: +33 (0)1 42 78 78 28
(see pages 76–79, 98–99)
An interior designer and collector of contemporary art, Méchiche supervises projects throughout the world with rigor and a keen sense of esthetics and function.

JEAN-MICHEL WILMOTTE
68, rue du Faubourg-Saint-Antoine
75012 Paris
Tel.: +33 (0)1 53 02 22 22
(see pages 58–63)
A graduate of the Camondo school and now a practicing architect, Wilmotte is a perfectionist whose designs are disciplined, clear-cut, and inventive. He works with flair on every continent in the world, adding a contemporary touch to historic buildings.

VAR

RUDY RICCIOTTI
3, place d'Estienne-d'Orves
83150 Bandol
Tel.: +33 (0)4 94 29 52 61
(see pages 60, 64–67)
The understated and innovative designs of this youthful architect from the Var (France)—a man who rejects regional clichés—are rooted in nature, while at the same time projecting a highly refined, minimalist spirit.

VAUCLUSE

HUGUES BOSC
38, boulevard Victor-Hugo
13210 Saint-Rémy
Tel.: +33 (0)4 90 92 10 81
(see pages 24–27, 31)
Specializing in the restoration and cellar-to-attic reconstruction of *mas* and *bastides*, Bosc modernizes old buildings, adding a contemporary note marked by elegance and balance.

LANDSCAPE ARCHITECTS

These talented men and women combine lessons learned from the past with total mastery of modern technology. They design paradisiacal gardens that enhance Provençal nature and its fragrant species, while offering a contemporary approach to landscape.

ALPES-MARITIMES

JEAN MUS
16, rue Frédéric-Mistral
06530 Cabris
Tel.: +33 (0)4 93 60 54 50
(see pages 12–13, 18–23)
Carefully orchestrated and installed with unrivaled mastery, the gardens designed by this native of Provence and great admirer of Ferdinand Bac seem derived solely from the sometimes slightly fanciful harmony of nature itself.

BOUCHES-DU-RHÔNE

DOMINIQUE LAFOURCADE

10, boulevard Mirabeau
13210 Saint-Rémy-de-
Provence
Tel.: +33 (0)4 90 92 10 14
Lafourcade designs her
gardens with an unerring
hand, drawing inspiration
from the principles of the
formal French gardens and
integrating them artfully
into the natural landscape.

MARC NUCERA
B.P. 16
13550 Noves
Tel.: +33 (0)4 90 92 99 21
This virtuoso landscape
sculptor arranges trees
and shrubs in patterns,
creating subtle
connections between
garden and countryside.
Combining the organic
and the mineral, Nucera
follows a principle of
formal harmony to
enhance the dynamic
personality of each
individual site and open
up sublime perspectives.
His is an analytical and
reflective art, through
which gardens become
visual compositions.

PARIS REGION

LOUIS BENECH
4, cité Saint-Chaumont
75019 Paris
Tel.: +33 (0)1 42 01 04 00
(see pages 8, 40–43, 46)
This fan of Provence has
designed numerous
gardens reflecting a
pragmatic approach to
landscape artistry, in
which formal rigor
determines the
arrangement of species

suitable to the local
climate and environment.

GILLES CLÉMENT
213, rue du Faubourg-
Saint-Antoine
75011 Paris
Tel.: +33 (0)1 43 48 59 24
(see pages 38–39)
Clément, who landscaped
the Domaine du Rayol, is
a globe-trotting artist in
perpetual motion—a
gardening revolutionary
who appreciates freedom
and the opportunity to
tackle virgin ground.
His vast spatial patterns
respect their terrain's
history, topography, and
native flora.

TARN

ARNAUD
MAURIÈRES ET
ERIC OSSART
Cordes-sur-Ciel
Avenue Paul-Bodin
81190 Tanus
Tel.: +33 (0)5 63 76 38 49
(see pages 34–37)
This partnership unites
two men who are
enterprising designers,
authors, and the guiding
spirits behind such admired
public projects as the Blois
parks. They also create
private gardens, including
the Alchemist's garden
described in the present
volume. They specialize in
the restoration of gardens
with legendary reputations.

VAUCLUSE

ALEX DINGWALL-
MAIN

Landscape Enterprise
84480 Lacoste
Tel.: +33 (0)4 90 75 92 32
(see pages 32–33)
This Scottish landscape
architect, author of an
original and idiosyncratic
book describing his new
life in Provence, currently
works imaginatively using
the native Provençal
countryside as a starting
point. Drawing on his
extensive knowledge of
local flora, he creates
consistently poetic designs
featuring rivers of lavender
and boxwood mazes.

MICHEL SÉMINI
Rue Saint-Frusquin
84220 Goult
Tel.: +33 (0)4 90 72 38 50
(see pages 24–28)
This landscape architect,
responsible for some of
the most elegant gardens
in the Vaucluse region,
believes that formal
designs should follow the
natural contours of the
local topography. Whether
intimate or grandiose, his
gardens seem to harmonize
perfectly with their sites
and the personalities of
their owners.

DECORATION
AND
TABLEWARE

*With meticulous attention to
authenticity and quality, but
without ostentation, these
charming and imaginative
shops display offer a new
type of Provençal lifestyle
with an eclectic choice of*

*decorative accessories, china,
fabrics, pottery, and cookware.*

ALPES-MARITIMES

FRAGONARD
MAISON
2, rue Amiral-de-Grasse
06130 Grasse
Tel.: +33 (0)4 93 36 44 65
(see page 167)
Fragonard's new line of
home products includes
china and hand-
embroidered linens in
classic Provençal and
attractive contemporary
designs, plus a selection of
very elegant accessories.

JACQUELINE
MORABITO
42–44, rue Yves-Klein
06480 La-Colle-sur-Loup
Tel.: +33 (0)4 93 32 64 91
(see pages 88–91, 167)
Jacqueline Morabito—
stylist, decorator, silver-
smith, sculptor—also
designs furniture,
household linens, and
ravishing accessories with
elegant understatement.

LA VERRERIE
DE BIOT
5, chemin des Combes
06410 Biot
Tel.: +33 (0)4 93 65 03 00
Blister-glass in pale colors
hand-crafted by master
glass-makers, and a fine
range of practical objects
such as carafes, cruets, and
decorative accessories.

BOUCHES-DU-RHÔNE

ÉBÈNE
38, boulevard Victor-Hugo

13210 Saint-Rémy-de-
Provence
Tel.: +33 (0)4 90 92 36 10
Displayed in the typically
Provençal setting of an old
olive mill are lap robes,
table linens, picture
frames, lamp globes,
collectibles, cushions,
pottery, a wide range of
lighting fixtures, embossed
fabrics, custom-trimmed
rugs and carpets, and
updated versions of
contemporary furniture.
Everything for decorating
the house.

LE GRAND
MAGASIN
24, rue de la Commune
13210 Saint-Rémy-de-
Provence
Tel.: +33 (0)4 90 92 18 79
This treasure-trove of
twentieth-century design
is a display case for
unusual young stylists
and artists. Among other
delights, it offers a
remarkable collection of
French and American
jewelry and accessories
from the 1950s through
the present.

POTERIE RAVEL
Avenue des Goums
13400 Aubagne
Tel.: +33 (0)4 42 32 07 27
Traditional culinary
earthenware in warm
colors. Tableware and
garden urns.

GARD

LA MAISON
D'UZÈS
8, rue du Docteur-

Blanchard
30700 Uzès
Tel.: +33 (0)6 11 33 38 43
Fax: +33 (0)6 09 66 47 51
The salons of this
eighteenth-century town
house contain a vast range
of decorative objects for
the home: antiques, fabrics,
old-fashioned bathroom
accessories, garden
fountains and vases, marbles
and statues, stone sinks. A
display on the upper floor
includes over 1,000 pieces
of antique Provence and
Languedoc pottery, most of
them practical objects
made of glazed terra-cotta.

NAVARRO ET
SABATIER
20, rue Persil
30300 Beaucaire
Tel.: +33 (0)4 90 72 36 84
Cane- and rush-bottom
Provençal chairs, hand-
crafted according to
traditional methods
in walnut, beech, and
painted wood.

POTERIE
D'ANDUZE
Les Enfants de Boisset
Route de St-Jean-du-Gard
30140 Anduze
Tel.: +33 (0)4 66 61 80 86
(see pages 40–43,
108–109)
The traditionally crafted
Anduze vases, which are
still the glory of parks
and gardens in the South
of France.

VAR

VALÉRIE
DEBUISSON

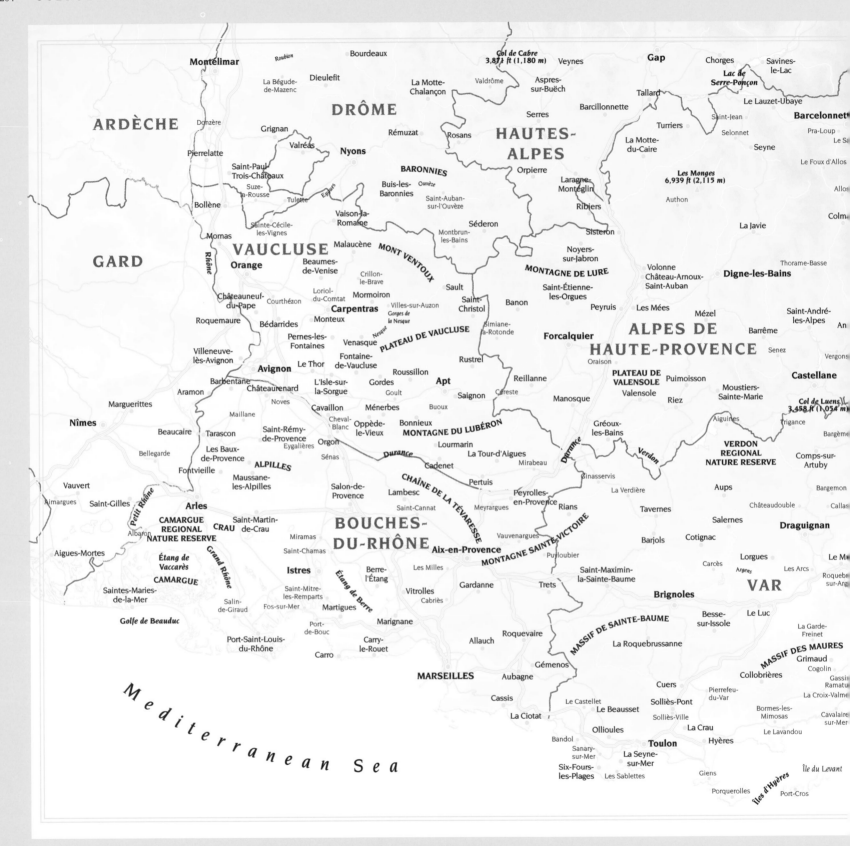

Montélimar
Roubion
Bourdeaux
Col de Cabre
3,871 ft (1,180 m)
Veynes
Gap
Chorges
Savines-
le-Lac
Lac de
Serre-Ponçon
La Bégude-
de-Mazenc
Dieulefit
La Motte-
Chalançon
Valdrôme
Aspres-
sur-Buëch
Tallard
Le Lauzet-Ubaye
Barcelonnet
DRÔME
HAUTES-
ALPES
ARDÈCHE
Donzère
Grignan
Rémuzat
Rosans
Serres
Barcillonnette
Turriers
Saint-Jean
Selonnet
Pra-Loup
Le Sa
Pierrelatte
Valréas
Nyons
BARONNIES
Orpierre
La Motte-
du-Caire
Seyne
Le Foux d'Allos
Saint-Paul-
Trois-Châteaux
Suze-
la-Rousse
Ouvèze
Buis-les-
Baronnies
Saint-Auban-
sur-l'Ouvèze
Laragne-
Montéglin
Les Monges
6,939 ft (2,115 m)
Authon
Allos
Bollène
Tulette
Eygues
Vaison-la-
Romaine
Montbrun-
les-Bains
Séderon
Ribiers
Sisteron
La Javie
Colm
GARD
Mornas
Sainte-Cécile-
les-Vignes
Malaucène
MONT VENTOUX
Noyers-
sur-Jabron
Volonne
Château-Arnoux-
Saint-Auban
Digne-les-Bains
Thorame-Basse
VAUCLUSE
Rhône
Orange
Beaumes-
de-Venise
Crillon-
le-Brave
Sault
MONTAGNE DE LURE
Saint-Étienne-
les-Orgues
La Javie
Châteauneuf-
du-Pape
Courthézon
Loriol-
du-Comtat
Mormoiron
Villes-sur-Auzon
Saint-
Christol
Banon
Peyruis
Les Mées
Mézel
Saint-André-
les-Alpes
Roquemaure
Bédarrides
Carpentras
Monteux
Gorges de
la Nesque
Nesque
Simiane-
la-Rotonde
Forcalquier
ALPES DE
HAUTE-PROVENCE
Barrême
Senez
Vergons
Villeneuve-
lès-Avignon
Pernes-les-
Fontaines
Venasque
PLATEAU DE VAUCLUSE
Rustrel
Reillanne
Oraison
PLATEAU DE
VALENSOLE
Puimoisson
Castellane
Aramon
Avignon
Le Thor
Fontaine-
de-Vaucluse
Roussillon
Apt
Saignon
Céreste
Manosque
Valensole
Riez
Moustiers-
Sainte-Marie
Col de Luens
3,458 ft (1,054 m
Barbentane
Châteaurenard
L'Isle-sur-
la-Sorgue
Gordes
Goult
Buoux
Gréoux-
les-Bains
Aiguines
Trigance
Bargèm
Margueritttes
Noves
Cavaillon
Ménerbes
Bonnieux
MONTAGNE DU LUBÉRON
Lourmarin
VERDON
REGIONAL
NATURE RESERVE
Comps-sur-
Artuby
Nîmes
Beaucaire
Tarascon
Saint-Rémy-
de-Provence
Cheval-
Blanc
Oppède-
le-Vieux
La Tour-d'Aigues
Mirabeau
Durance
Verdon
Bellegarde
Les Baux-
de-Provence
Eygalières
Orgon
Sénas
Durance
Cadenet
Pertuis
Binasservis
La Verdière
Aups
Bargemon
Callas
Fontvieille
ALPILLES
Vauvert
Maussane-
les-Alpilles
Salon-de-
Provence
Lambesc
CHAÎNE DE LA TRÉVARESSE
Peyrolles-
en-Provence
Rians
Meyrargues
Tavernes
Salernes
Châteaudouble
Draguignan
Aimargues
Saint-Gilles
Arles
Saint-Martin-
de-Crau
Miramas
BOUCHES-
DU-RHÔNE
Saint-Cannat
Vauvenargues
MONTAGNE SAINTE-VICTOIRE
Barjols
Cotignac
Lorgues
Carcès
Le M
CAMARGUE
REGIONAL
NATURE RESERVE
CRAU
Saint-Chamas
Aix-en-Provence
Puyloubier
Les Arcs
Roqu
sur-Arg
Albaron
Étang de
Vaccarès
Grand Rhône
Istres
Étang de Berre
Berre-
l'Étang
Les Milles
Gardanne
Trets
Saint-Maximin-
la-Sainte-Baume
Brignoles
Argens
VAR
Saintes-Maries-
de-la-Mer
CAMARGUE
Salin-
de-Giraud
Saint-Mitre-
les-Remparts
Martigues
Vitrolles
Cabriès
MASSIF DE SAINTE-BAUME
Besse-
sur-Issole
Le Luc
La Garde-
Freinet
Golfe de Beauduc
Fos-sur-Mer
Port-
de-Bouc
Marignane
Roquevaire
La Roquebrussanne
MASSIF DES MAURES
Grimaud
Gassi
Ramatu
Port-Saint-Louis-
du-Rhône
Carry-
le-Rouet
Marseilles
Aubagne
Allauch
Gémenos
Cuers
Pierrefeu-
du-Var
Collobrières
Cogolin
La Croix-Valme
Carro
MARSEILLES
Cassis
Le Castellet
Solliès-Pont
Bormes-les-
Mimosas
Cavalaire-
sur-Mer
La Ciotat
Le Beausset
Solliès-Ville
La Crau
Le Lavandou
Ollioules
Bandol
Sanary-
sur-Mer
Toulon
Hyères
Six-Fours-
les-Plages
La Seyne-
sur-Mer
Les Sablettes
Giens
Île du Levant
Porquerolles
Îles d'Hyères
Port-Cros
Mediterranean Sea

ITALY

MONTAGNE DE L'ALP

Saint-Paul-sur-Ubaye

Larche

Jausiers

Saint-Étienne-
de-Tinée

Auron

Tunnel de Tende

MERCANTOUR
NATIONAL PARK

Beuil

Saint-Martin-
Vésubie

Tende

Guillaumes

Valberg

Saint-Sauveur-
sur-Tinée

La Brigue

ALPES
MARITIMES

Roquebillière

Saorge

Lantosque

Entrevaux

Puget-Théniers

Utelle

Peira-Cava

Breil-sur-Roya

Sospel

Roquesteron

Levens

L'Escarène

L'Esteron

Saint-Auban

Montagne
du Cheiron
5,833 ft (1,778 m)

Le Loup

Contes

Gorbio

Coursegoules

La Turbie

Menton
Monte-Carlo
Monaco

Vence

Beaulieu-
sur-Mer

Saint-Vallier-
de-Thiey

Le Bar-
sur-Loup

Tourrettes-
sur-Loup

Saint-
Paul

Nice

Saint-Jean-Cap-Ferrat

Villefranche-
sur-Mer

Grasse

Biot

Cagnes-
sur-Mer

Fayence

Le Plan-
de-Grasse

Plascassier

La Brague

Mougins

Vallauris

Antibes

Le Cannet

Juan-les-Pins

Mandelieu-
la-Napoule

Cannes

ESTÉREL

Miramar

Côte d'Azur

Fréjus

Agay

Saint-Raphaël

Saint-Aygulf

Sainte-
Maxime

Saint-Tropez

0   20 km

© carte : Edigraphie

Route de Lac
83590 Carcès
Tel.: +33 (0)4 94 04 37 33
One of the last tinsmiths
still at work can be
found here, in the
lovely village of Carcès.
Plates, platters, soup
tureens, ramekins, as
well as candelabra can
be made to order using
antique molds.

**POTERIE DU
CHÂTEAU**
Route de Draguignan
Quartier Saint-Romain
83690 Salernes
Tel.: +33 (0)4 94 70 63 46
Glazed baking dishes and
bowls. Roof, ridge, and
gutter tiles. A real treasure-
trove for all terra-cotta fans.

VAUCLUSE

GÉRARD AUDE
Saint-Pantaléon
84220 Gordes
Tel.: +33 (0)4 90 72 22 67
Superb wrought-iron
pieces—furniture, arbors,
and pergolas designed to
create a dream setting
outdoors in the garden, or
to add a special touch to a
romantic winter garden
created indoors.

**ATELIERS
LAFFANOUR**
91, avenue de la
Libération
84150 Jonquières
Tel.: +33 (0)4 90 70 60 82
Traditionally crafted chairs
and armchairs in a variety
of styles. Round, oval, and
rectangular tables, and
table extensions. Coffee

tables. Fireside chairs
made from walnut for
waxing or from plane-tree
wood for painting.

HERVÉ BAUME
19–19 ter, rue Petite-
Fusterie
84000 Avignon
Tel.: +33 (0)4 90 86 37 66
In a setting of refined
elegance, Hervé Baume
specializes in unusual
furnishings and accessories
from every period. He
also offers a line of garden
furniture that can be
made to order.

CÔTÉ BASTIDE
3, rue du Grand Pré
84160 Lourmarin
Tel.: +33 (0)4 90 08 57 92
(see page 9)
In an authentic and
romantic setting,
Houques displays a few
elegantly rustic pieces of
furniture and a line of
household linens, china,
and bath products. The
tableware comes in a
subtly monochromatic
color range.

**ÉTABLISSEMENT
FAUCON**
286, avenue de la
Libération
84400 Apt
Tel.: +33 (0)4 90 74 15 31
For six generations this
firm has upheld the
ancient tradition of
blended earthenware
made with a skillful mix
of different raw clays.
Elegant shades of blue,
pink, and green
complement the classic

yellow and brown tones.
A selection of bowls, soup
tureens, and serving
dishes, decorated with
patterns of foliage, fruit,
or human figures,
completes this line of
tableware, which has a
decidedly baroque spirit.

HOM LE XUAN
84220 Lumières
Tel.: +33 (0)4 90 72 36 84
Cell phone: +33 (0)6 08
23 68 70
Displayed in a soothing
atmosphere, cleanly
designed furniture
combining iron, wood,
and zinc that expresses a
skillful balance between
East and West.

**MARTINE GILLES
ET JAAP WIEMAN**
84390 Brantes
Tel.: +33 (0)4 75 28 03 37
A ceramics studio offering
creations of great charm,
including tableware
decorated with tiny
romantic flowers.

**LE MAS DE
CUREBOURG**
Route d'Apt
84800 L'Isle-sur-la-Sorgue
Tel.: +33 (0)4 90 20 30 06
Fine Provençal furniture,
including rush-bottom
chairs and armchairs, plus
reproductions of
traditional pieces painted
in pastel shades.

EDITH MÉZARD
Château de l'Ange
84220 Lumières
Tel.: +33 (0)4 90 72 36 41
(see page 86)

On display in a fine old farmhouse adjoining a manor, it is easy to be seduced by this appealing line of household linens; cashmere, cotton, and linen clothing, and ravishing decorative accessories, which are all understated and refined.

SACHA DÉCORATION

Place Albert-Roure
84560 Ménerbes
Tel.: +33 (0)4 90 72 41 38
Using eighteenth-century materials, Lionel and Sacha Houant restore the soul to antique furnishings, in order to create atmospheric settings without parallel. Also notable for an elegant collection of antique pottery and Provençal bedspreads.

TERRE E PROVENCE

26, rue de la République
84000 Avignon
Tel.: +33 (0)4 90 85 56 45
or +33 (0)4 90 16 52 52
Crafted according to traditional methods in Dieulefit, this line of tableware in simple forms and strong colors (blue, yellow, green) also includes baking dishes, jars, carafes, and the traditional omelette turner.

VOX POPULI

54, rue Joseph-Vernet
84000 Avignon
Tel.: +33 (0)4 90 85 70 25
Pascale Palun's

housewares, furniture, and lighting fixtures are highly individual additions to any interior. Palun designs original and inspiring items using antique and recycled materials.

ANTIQUE AND SECOND-HAND DEALERS

Informed connoisseurs may choose to attend auctions held by antique dealers on specific dates in Aix, Antibes, Cannes, Marseilles, Monaco, and Saint-Tropez, but browsing in the flea markets of Uzès, Lignane, Marseilles, and Nice represents one of the great pleasures of Provence.

L'Isle-sur-la-Sorgue occupies a special place in the hearts of treasure-hunters. Every weekend, along the banks of the Sorgue, second-hand dealers display unusual furniture and accessories— both practical and frivolous— from all over the world. In addition to these temporary flea-market stands, the town also contains ravishing clusters of shops, including the Quai de la Gare, Village des Antiquaires de la Gare, Isle aux Brocantes, Espace Béchard, Hôtel Dongier, Rives de la Sorgue, Cour de François, and Rendez-Vous des Marchands—all exciting stops on the treasure-hunter's itinerary.

The finest and most valuable furniture and accessories are found primarily in shops run by

antique dealers. Usually specializing in a specific period, these dealers are among the foremost defenders of the local heritage, sharing with others their reverence for the artists and artisans of Provence.

ALPES-MARITIMES

LEI NOUESTREI VIEI

614, route de la Mer
06410 Biot
Tel.: +33 (0)4 93 65 02 05
An antique shop specializing in folk art. A fine collection of garden urns and earthenware items for the kitchen.

BOUCHES-DU-RHÔNE

FÉLIX-AILHAUD

35, rue Cardinale
13100 Aix-en-Provence
Tel.: +33 (0)4 42 27 96 69
In the heart of Aix's old city, a selection of ravishing antique furniture and some fine reproductions— including dressers, loveseats, consoles, and patinated wooden moldings.

L'ANTIQUAIRE DE MAUSSANE

Bastide Saint Bastien
99, avenue de la Vallée-des-Baux
13520 Maussane
Tel.: +33 (0)4 90 54 37 64
Visitors to this magnificent nineteenth-century residence will find a collection of seventeenth-and eighteenth-century furniture from the South of France, in walnut, elm,

and fruitwood, as well as eighteenth-century painted wooden furniture, rush-bottom chairs, antique faïence, paintings by Provençal artists, and decorative accessories.

VAR

LES MILLE ET UNE PORTES

Place Émile-Zola
83570 Carcès
Tel.: +33 (0)4 94 04 50 27
A large range of antique doors, and furniture from the seventeenth and eighteenth centuries.

PATRICE POTIER

La Jumenterie de Bagateau
83570 Carcès
Tel./Fax: +33 (0)4 94 04 31 75
Cell phone: +33 (0)6 84 20 39 95
A superb display of folding garden furniture from the nineteenth century and the "Gay Nineties"—the 1900s. Of special note: an extraordinary *balancelle*.

VAUCLUSE

MICHEL BIEHN

7, avenue des Quatre-Otages
84800 L'Isle-sur-la-Sorgue
Tel.: +33 (0)4 90 20 89 04
(see pages 162–163, 165, 168–169)
This connoisseur and author of books on Provence offers a range of antique fabrics—including embossed and quilted

varieties—plus an impressive selection of fabrics from the Middle East and the Orient, complemented by a selection of decorative accessories chosen with wit and unerring taste.

BERTRAND COLOMBIER ET BRUNO DION

7, avenue des Quatre-Otages
84800 L'Isle-sur-la-Sorgue
Tel.: +33 (0)4 90 38 62 95
Ceramics in dazzling colors.

L'ISLE AUX BROCANTES

7 avenue des Quatre-Otages
84800 L'Isle-sur-la-Sorgue
Tel.: +33 (0)4 90 20 73 55
Jean Lacour is interested in the mineral world: statues and garden urns, obelisks, flameware. He also offers finely crafted furniture, theatrical sets, navigational instruments, and other unusual objects.

VILLAGE DES ANTIQUAIRES

84800 L'Isle-sur-la-Sorgue
Tel.: +33 (0)4 90 38 04 57/20 38
An appealing spot where weekend browsers will find delightful antique furniture and accessories.

VINCENT-MIT-L'ÂNE

Route d'Apt
84800 L'Isle-sur-la-Sorgue
Jean-Jacques Bourgeois, author of *L'Âge d'or du siège paillé* ("The Golden Age of

the Rush-bottom Chair"), specializes in seventeenth-century Provençal antiques: pottery, tableware, chairs, and occasional furniture.

GERMAIN ELENA

Quartier Saint-Julien
30, boulevard Charles-Gide
84000 Avignon
Tel.: +33 (0)4 66 03 19 36
Antiques, collectibles, paintings, gilded wood, period frames. The focus is on the eighteenth century.

GÉRARD GUERRE

1, Plan de Lunel
84000 Avignon
Tel.: +33 (0)4 90 86 42 67
(see pages 165, 170–171)
Visitors to the imposing Les Laurens town house will find gilded carved wood, mirrors, and looking-glasses arranged beside magnificent examples of antique furnishings and accessories from the seventeenth and eighteenth centuries. Guerre's seminal book, *Les Arts décoratifs en Provence du XVIIIe au XIXe* ("The Decorative Arts in Provence in the Eighteenth and Nineteenth Century"), should be on everyone's reading list.

JEAN-PIERRE MAGNAN

8 bis, rue Mazeau
84100 Orange
Tel.: +33 (0)4 90 34 25 62
Finely crafted and restored

Provençal furniture and musical instruments, including three-holed flutes, tambourines, spinets, stringed tambourines, psalteries, bachas, and fifes—all made from fruitwood and other exquisite varieties such as walnut, Brazilian rosewood, and ebony.

LE MAS DE FLORE
84800 Lagnes
Tel.: +33 (0)4 90 20 37 96
Pierre Degrugillier offers fine walnut furniture and antique objects evoking the history of Provence. In his workshop next door, he uses traditional regional methods to produce new furniture.

CAFÉS AND TEA ROOMS

Every village in Provence boasts a café terrace waiting to welcome strollers under its plane trees. Taking a break in the shade and nibbling on a regional specialty are part of the enjoyment of any trip. Below are a few suggestions, among many possibilities, of places where our readers can linger for a moment and savor the charm of these exceptional places.

ALPES-MARITIMES

LE CAFÉ DES MUSÉES
1, rue Jean-Ossola
06130 Grasse
Tel.: +33 (0)4 92 60 99 00
(see page 164)

Directly across from the Fragonard Museum and the ravishing Museum of Jewelry and Costume, a restaurant/tea room designed by Agnès and Françoise Costa in conjunction with Jacqueline Morabito. Gourmet treats are served under the arbor on the terrace or in the cool little room inside. Ingredients are fresh from the market, and on offer are delicious desserts including biscuits d'Hélène and delectably crisp sand tarts—made from an old family recipe, of course.

VILLA-MUSÉE EPHRUSSI DE ROTHSCHILD
06290 Saint-Jean-Cap-Ferrat
Tel.: +33 (0)4 93 01 33 09
Visitors to this former Chinese salon can admire the Villefranche bay while enjoying a light lunch. An elegant, delightful spot that should not be missed.

MUSÉE DES ARTS ASIATIQUES
405, promenade des Anglais
06200 Nice
Tel.: +33 (0)4 92 29 37 00
An exotic spot—designed by the great architect Kenzo Tange—in which to enjoy a cup of tea. On Sundays a master of the tea ceremony demonstrates the subtleties of this highly symbolic art. Reservations required.

BOUCHES-DU-RHÔNE

CAFÉ-BASTIDE DU COURS
43, 45, 47 cours Mirabeau
13100 Aix-en-Provence
Tel.: +33 (0)4 42 26 55 41
A historic residence in the eighteenth-century Provençal farmhouse style, restored and decorated by Roland Le Bévillon and Maurice Savinel and located halfway down the Cours Mirabeau. Provençal specialties are served on the sumptuous terrace, and in the salons adjoining the manor and the library. Guests are accommodated in five elegant bedrooms (including two suites) dedicated to famed Provençal painters—including Paul Cézanne, of course. Its relaxed and pleasurable atmosphere ensures a loyal clientele.

LE GRILLON
49, cours Mirabeau
13100 Aix-en-Provence
Tel.: +33 (0)4 42 27 58 81
Customers can enjoy a drink on the lively terrace, or varied and renowned cuisine in the dining room, appealingly decorated by Gilles Dez. A brasserie with an irresistible atmosphere.

LES DEUX-GARÇONS
53, cours Mirabeau
13100 Aix-en-Provence
Tel.: +33 (0)4 42 26 00 51
This café with the gilt paneling is an Aix institution, frequented in

the eighteenth century by Mirabeau himself. Today, the crowded terrace is filled in summertime with the city's gilded youth and music lovers visiting Aix for the festival. Lunch and dinner are served in the First Empire dining room, a listed monument.

VAUCLUSE

LE GRAND CAFÉ
Cour Maria-Casarès
84000 Avignon
Tel.: +33 (0)4 90 86 86 77
This café's loft-style dining room welcomes film buffs and patrons of the city's theater festival. Its terrace is a fashionable meeting-place in summer. Recommended: the high-quality Mediterranean cuisine served with style at reasonable prices.

RESTAURANTS WITH EXCEPTIONAL CHARM

Selected for their romantic settings and the quality of their cuisine, the following restaurants have gained approval from a demanding clientele of gourmets who appreciate a warm welcome and fresh ingredients.

ALPES-DE-HAUTE-PROVENCE

LA BASTIDE DE MOUSTIERS
04360 Moustiers-Sainte-Marie

Tel.: +33 (0)4 92 70 47 47
When Alain Ducasse succumbed to the charm of this farmhouse in Moustiers, he naturally enough turned to youthful, loyal, and talented chef Vincent Maillard to head the new enterprise. Served in a warm terra-cotta and pastel setting, Maillard's cuisine features regional dishes based on garden produce, as well as Provençal herbs, of course.

LE LAPIN TANT PIS
10, avenue Saint-Promasse
04300 Forcalquier
Tel.: +33 (0)4 92 75 38 88
Both inside his restaurant—a converted residence once occupied by the town blacksmith—and outside, at elegant tables under the trees, Gérard Vives serves an inventive version of Provençal cuisine enhanced by his own inspiration. Drawing on the flavors of exotic spices, aromatic herbs, and crisp vegetables, Vives offers brilliant and delicious demonstrations of his demanding culinary philosophy.

OLIVIER AND CO
3, rue des Cordeliers
04300 Forcalquier
Tel.: +33 (0)4 92 75 00 75
A shop dedicated to olive oil and all the other products of the olive tree, combined with a friendly and cheerful restaurant. Recipes with a strong Mediterranean character

contribute to a menu with a decidedly gourmet slant that changes every day.

ALPES-MARITIMES

LE MOULIN DE MOUGINS
424, chemin du Moulin
06250 Mougins
Tel.: +33 (0)4 93 75 78 24
In wintertime, Roger and Denise Vergé cultivate gastronomy and the good life inside their romantic mill. In the summer, they move to the sculpture garden outside.

BOUCHES-DU-RHÔNE

CENTRE VILLE
65, avenue de la Vallée-des-Baux
13520 Maussane-les-Alpilles
Tel.: +33 (0)4 90 54 23 31
In a Provençal setting updated by the artists of Couleurs du Temps, the Démery family (Jean-Pierre, Christine, Christian, Stéphanie) have perfected a cuisine that is based on the best products available in their local market. The menu offers seasonal, typically Provençal dishes as well as Italian specialties.

LES ARCENAULX
25, cours d'Estienne-d'Orves
13000 Marseilles
Tel.: +33 (0)4 91 59 80 30
In this port that formerly sheltered slave-galleys, the bookstore and restaurant

run by Jeanne and Simone Laffitte has made a major contribution to the region's literary renaissance. The couple continue to offer their winning combination of culture and gastronomy, a convivial atmosphere in which customers can browse, buy, and enjoy simple and tasty meals.

LA CHASSAGNETTE
Route de Sambuc
13200 Arles
Tel.: +33 (0)4 90 97 26 86
In this old, tastefully decorated Camargue farmhouse, guests enjoy delicious meals featuring flowers the chef picks from the garden himself. In summertime, dinner is served outside under an arbor; guests can watch cattle grazing on the farm next door.

CHEZ BRU
Rue de la République
13810 Eygalières
Tel.: +33 (0)4 90 90 60 34
A village bistro serving refined and creative cuisine in a delightful setting that displays a harmonious blend of exposed stone, painted wood, and crisp linens.

CHEZ MIREILLE DESANA
13460 Saintes-Maries-de-la-Mer
Tel.: +33 (0)4 90 97 72 15
(see pages 134–135)
Dining at this table d'hôte in the heart of the Camargue is by reservation

only, with special rates for groups of eight or more. The unique setting was designed by the owner, specialist in driftwood furniture. The menu features a dozen or so typically Mediterranean dishes. Guests plan their meals by phone when making their reservation.

LE BISTROT DES ALPILLES
15, boulevard Mirabeau
13210 Saint-Rémy
Tel.: +33 (0)4 90 92 09 17
A warm, typically Provençal setting, popular with both Parisian connoisseurs and local residents. Ideal for sampling such regional specialties as braised lamb, stuffed vegetables, artichokes barigoule, sardines escabèche, eggplant Provençal, and so on.

LA COUR DE ROHAN
10, rue Vauvenargues
13100 Aix-en-Provence
Tel.: +33 (0)4 42 96 18 15
This tea room in a ravishing seventeenth-century town house serves light lunches in an attractive interior courtyard. The menu features a selection of salads, delectable homemade pastries, and more than twenty varieties of tea.

LE BISTROT DU PARADOU
57, avenue de la Vallée-de-la-Baux

13520 Le Paradou
Tel.: +33 (0)4 90 54 32 70
Fine Provençal cuisine based on fresh ingredients from the market and the fisherman's latest catch: aïoli at noon on Fridays, soupe au pistou in summertime, pot-au-feu and daube in winter, goat's cheese and homemade desserts. Friendly atmosphere guaranteed.

PÉRON
56, corniche Kennedy
13007 Marseilles
Tel.: +33 (0)4 91 52 15 22
Nestled against the rock opposite the Château d'If, a 1940s-style cruise-ship decor featuring mahogany, marble, and dark exotic woods lends a supremely chic note to this spot that has been updated and restored by Roger Misraki. The menu offers extremely fresh and flavorful seafood dishes, including a bouillabaisse famous in the region.

VAR

HOSTELLERIE DE L'ABBAYE DE LA CELLE
Place du Général-de-Gaulle
83170 La Celle
Tel.: +33 (0)4 98 05 14 14
The second hotel-restaurant opened by Alain Ducasse, in an imposing eighteenth-century manor house, is supervised by Bruno Clément—a truffle specialist with a strong

personality. The authentic flavor of traditional cuisine can be found here. Cooking courses are available.

VAUCLUSE

LA PETITE MAISON
Place de l'Étang
84160 Cucuron
Tel.: +33 (0)4 90 77 18 60
Drawing on his grandmother's recipes, chef Michel Medhi changes his delectable menu daily. There are four basic seasonal menus: the Black Truffle Menu for winter, the Asparagus and Tender Morels Menu for Spring, the White Truffle Menu for summer, and the Mushroom-and-Game Menu for autumn. The poolside setting surrounded by shady plane trees is a treat for the eye.

LE FOURNIL
5, place Carnot
84480 Bonnieux
Tel.: +33 (0)4 90 75 83 62
A cave-like terraced restaurant on the village square. The baker's oven carved into the rock is worthy of note. Le Fournil's regional cuisine, based on fresh products, is highly popular with all lovers of Provence.

MAS TOURTERON
Les Imberts
Chemin de Saint-Blaise
84220 Gordes
Tel.: +33 (0)4 90 72 09 81

Elizabeth Bourgeois plays hostess in the intimate atmosphere of this attractively decorated private residence with a romantic garden. Highly individual cuisine based on regional recipes heightened with—why not?—Indian spices.

HOTELS WITH EXCEPTIONAL CHARM

The following list cannot possibly do justice to the many charming hotels in Provence and on the Côte d'Azur. It includes only those establishments that members of our team have visited in person, or those that trusted advisers living in the region have recommended. These hotels have retained their authenticity while adapting to the demands of modern life. They make no attempt to vie with more luxurious hostelries, and are focused on a single goal: to delight their guests by offering them the subtleties of a beguiling lifestyle.

ALPES-DE-HAUTE-PROVENCE

LA BASTIDE DE MOUSTIERS
04360 Moustiers-Sainte-Marie
Tel.: +33 (0)4 92 70 47 47
At a nod from Alain Ducasse, each of the rooms in this hotel were given an individual color, atmosphere, and image of

Provence— reflected in their names: Sunflower, Lavender, Raspberry, and so on. The distinctive style of each room extends to the smallest details, and even to the adjoining bathrooms.

ALPES-MARITIMES

HÔTEL WINDSOR
11, rue Dalpozzo
06000 Nice
Tel.: +33 (0)4 93 88 59 35
An oasis of greenery in the center of Nice, the Hôtel Windsor offers—in addition to its swimming pool ringed by tropical plants—a dozen or so rooms that have been individually decorated by renowned contemporary artists. The Nice School of artists is, of course, well represented here!

LA COLOMBE D'OR
Place du Général-de-Gaulle
06570 Saint-Paul-de-Vence
Tel.: +33 (0)4 93 32 80 02
Few experiences are more enjoyable than staying at this combined inn and museum that is filled with paintings by great twentieth-century masters such as Braque, Picasso, and Miró; dining in the Roman garden next to a large ceramic sculpture by Léger; and reviving the memory of famous names in literature and politics, on stage and screen. Comfortable bedrooms overlook either the valley

or the square—where traditional games of pétanque are still played.

HÔTEL BELLES-RIVES
33, bd Édouard-Baudoin
06160 Antibes-Juan-Les-Pins
Tel.: +33 (0)4 93 61 02 79
(see pages 180–181)
One of the few great hotels on the Côte d'Azur with a terrace directly overlooking the sea. It is also one of the last surviving examples on Cap d'Antibes of the resort architectural style of the 1930s. Scott Fitzgerald loved the terrace of this luxurious establishment.

LE CHÂTEAU DES OLLIÈRES
39, avenue des Baumettes
06000 Nice
Tel.: +33 (0)4 92 15 77 99
(see page 179)
With its old-fashioned splendor and flower-filled park, the Château des Ollières hotel—formerly the residence of Prince Lobanov-Rostovsky—evokes Nice's early twentieth-century golden age. The salons distill an atmosphere that is both intimate and luxurious.

L'HÔTEL DES DEUX FRÈRES
Place des Deux-Frères
06190 Roquebrune
Tel.: +33 (0)4 93 28 99 00
This hotel at the foot of a tenth-century château offers ten distinctive rooms, each decorated according to a specific theme—Moroccan, African, Bridal-Suite. Summertime meals on the terrace with a magnificent view of the Mediterranean are magical.

LE MAS CANDILLE
Bd Clément-Rebuffel
06250 Mougins
Tel.: +33 (0)4 92 28 43 43
This old eighteenth-century farmhouse nestled in the greenery above Cannes contains twenty ravishing bedrooms and a gourmet restaurant. A calm, peaceful atmosphere reigns around the two swimming pools. A Shiseido Spa is scheduled to open soon.

LE ROYAL RIVIERA
3, avenue Jean-Monnet
06230 Saint-Jean-Cap-Ferrat
Tel.: +33 (0)4 93 76 31 00
This small, newly renovated luxury hotel located midway between Nice and Monaco and overlooking the Mediterranean was built in the early twentieth century. Its chic and elegant bar has become a fashionable local meeting-place. Private beach; large, well-heated swimming pool; exquisite bedrooms. Garden recently redesigned by Jean Mus.

BOUCHES-DU-RHÔNE

CHÂTEAU DE ROUSSAN
N 99, about a mile after St-Rémy, in the direction of Tarascon
13210 Saint-Rémy de Provence
Tel.: +33 (0)4 90 92 11 63
One of the region's loveliest alleys of plane trees leads to this ravishing eighteenth-century château offering guests some twenty rooms with old-fashioned charm. The fifteen-acre park is a magical spot—swans drift on the water in the garden's interconnecting stone canals, statues are reflected in a Roman pool, and a nineteenth-century greenhouse hides behind lush shrubbery in the distance.

CHÂTEAU DES ALPILLES
Ancienne route des Baux, D 31, 13210 Saint-Rémy-de-Provence
Tel.: +33 (0)4 90 92 03 33
This fine nineteenth-century manor house nestled among the trees of a magnificent park, once welcomed such eminent guests as Chataubriand and Lamartine. Meticulously decorated in period style, the bedrooms are comfortable and the furnishings and colors confer a unique character on each one.

GRAND HÔTEL NORD-PINUS
Place du Forum
13200 Arles
Tel.: +33 (0)4 90 93 44 44
(see page 183)
In the historic heart of Arles, this hotel offers guests a nostalgic journey back to the ambience of salons from another age. A hotel with a soul that Jean Cocteau found utterly fascinating.

LE MAS DES ARNELLES
Avenue Arles
13460 Saintes-Maries-de-la-Mer
Tel.: +33 (0)4 90 97 61 59
(see page 182)
Decorated with elegant understatement, the bedrooms at the Arnelles are built on piles over the water, affording a view of the marshlands beyond. Its location, architecture, and stables make this timeless spot emblematic of the Camargue spirit.

LE MAS DE PEINT
Le Sambuc 13200 Arles
Tel.: +33 (0)4 90 97 20 62
Fax: +33 (0)4 90 97 22 20
Lucille and Jacques Bon are hosts at this luxurious hotel located in one wing of a seventeenth-century manor. Lucille, an architect, supervised the interior decoration, which features neutral colors and natural furnishings with a touch of sophistication. A perfect setting for enjoying meals that include savory meats, golden tarts, and the estate's own poultry and garden produce.

HÔTEL LE CORBUSIER
280, boulevard Michelet
13008 Marseilles
Tel.: +33 (0)4 91 77 18 15
Fax: +33 (0)4 91 16 78 28
This hotel is part of a residential unit built according to plans designed by Le Corbusier and based on this peerless architect's concept of efficient living space. The surprisingly spacious rooms overlooking the bay of Marseilles are now fifty years old. A few of them are fully equipped studio apartments. The hotel often serves as a conference and seminar center for architectural-arts scholars and students from all over the world.

LE MAS DE LA FOUQUE
Route du Petit-Rhône
13460 Saintes-Maries-de-la-Mer
Tel.: +33 (0)4 90 97 81 02
In the heart of the Camargue, a luxury hotel set against a stunningly wild natural backdrop. After an outing by foot or on horseback, guests return to enjoy a menu of house specialties served in elegant surroundings.

RELAIS DE LA MAGDELEINE
Chemin Jas-de-la-Lèbre
13420 Gémenos
Tel.: +33 (0)4 42 32 20 16
(see page 185)
Superb eighteenth-century farmhouse offering bedrooms and suites decorated with meticulous care. A collection of antique furnishings and paintings adorns the bedrooms and the little salons where an exquisite and delectable cuisine is served. The garden—with its pools, plane trees, and swimming pool—is a haven of cool shade.

VILLA CALANCO
27, avenue Victor-Hugo
13260 Cassis
Tel.: +33 (0)4 42 01 71 89
A spacious and extremely comfortable full-service apartment with a vast terrace overlooking the bay of Cassis. Direct access to the sea.

GARD

CHÂTEAU DE SAINT-MAXIMIN
Rue du Château
30700 Saint-Maximin
Tel.: +33 (0)4 66 03 44 16
Bedrooms and suites in the château's seventeenth-century wing—built by Racine's uncle, Canon Sconin—are painted in the warm tints of Provençal chalk. Breakfast is served under an arbor of solanum and jasmine facing ancient olive trees.

VAR

AUBERGE DES GLYCINES
22, place d'Armes
Île de Porquerolles
83400 Hyères
Tel.: +33 (0)4 94 58 30 36
On a village square open only to pedestrians and cyclists, this little Provençal inn smothered in bougainvillea offers a dreamlike setting. The eleven bedrooms behind their blue shutters could

not be more romantic. The equally fine restaurant is as popular with casual diners as with guests staying for the entire summer.

HOSTELLERIE DE L'ABBAYE DE LA CELLE

Place du Général-de-Gaulle
83170 La Celle
Tel.: +33 (0)4 98 05 14 14
This hotel between Cannes and Aix is another find by Alain Ducasse. Housed in an eighteenth-century Provençal building next to a Benedictine abbey, it now boasts some ten bedrooms, including three duplexes with private gardens, overlooking the experimental vineyards of the Maison des Vins des Coteaux Varois. Under Ducasse's supervision, the menu is as sumptuous as the decor. The accent is on Provençal specialties, and (of course) truffles in every possible form.

HOSTELLERIE DES GORGES DE PENNAFORT

About four miles southeast on the route du Muy
83830 Callas
Tel.: +33 (0)4 94 76 66 51
A recommended gourmet stop adjacent to the gulf of Saint-Tropez and not far from the Verdon gorges. The hospitality is warm and inviting, and owner-chef Da Silva's cuisine draws on the wealth of local flavors.

Sixteen very comfortable bedrooms in which dinner guests can prolong their enjoyment of the romantic little lake and the gorges.

HÔTEL SOULEIAS

Plage de Gigaro
83420 La Croix-Valmer
Tel.: +33 (0)4 94 55 10 55
The hotel's name means "sunny spot." This multi-level hotel, surrounded by grassy lawns and parasol pines, is perched on a wooded hill overlooking the Gigaro. Gourmet restaurant, heated pool, and a sixty-foot sailboat for sea excursions.

LE MANOIR

83400 Île de Port-Cros
Tel.: +33 (0)4 94 05 90 52
Surrounded by eucalyptus, rose laurels, and ancient palms, this fine residence with white turreted walls distills the tranquil charm of old-fashioned manor houses. Twenty bedrooms and apartments—some with private terrace and all with southern exposure—overlook a large, five-acre enclosed park that borders the sea. Garden swimming pool and rustic bar under the aromatic shade of eucalyptus trees.

VAUCLUSE

HOSTELLERIE DE CRILLON-LE-BRAVE

Place de l'Église
84410 Crillon-le-Brave

Tel.: +33 (0)4 90 65 61 61
(see page 184)
Bedrooms featuring Provençal fabric, salons decorated in the ocher tones characteristic of Rousillon soil, country-style Provençal warmth and comfort in a group of houses clustered around the village church.

HÔTEL DE L'ATELIER

5, rue de la Foire
30400 Villeneuve-lès-Avignon
Tel.: +33 (0)4 90 25 01 84
A charming sixteenth-century hotel. Small restaurant and tea room in the adjoining chapel, also sixteenth century.

HÔTEL DE LA MIRANDE

4, place Amirande
84000 Avignon
Tel.: +33 (0)4 90 85 93 93
(see pages 176–178)
At the foot of the Papal Palace stands a hotel that was once the luxurious residence of a cardinal. Restored ten years ago and furnished with antique furniture and collectors' items, it has now regained all of its eighteenth-century authenticity. An exceptional place to stay, offering refined cuisine created by renowned chefs and a range of high-quality services, including tours (by appointment only) of Provence's secret gardens, led by famed guide Louisa Jones, who has also written many books on gardens.

GUEST HOUSES

Reflecting current shifts in consumer attitudes and a revived quest for authenticity, guest houses have become increasingly popular with demanding travelers who appreciate warm hospitality in charming settings. A new way of exploring Provençal lifestyles from the inside.

ALPES-MARITIMES

BASTIDE DU BOSQUET

06160 Cap-d'Antibes
Tel.: +33 (0)4 93 67 32 29
Located between the cape and beaches of Antibes and Juan-les-Pins, this sun-drenched eighteenth-century farmhouse nestled among laurel and lotus trees offers three comfortable guest rooms with typical Provençal charm. Just a five-minute walk from the beach.

MAISON LACORDAIRE

466, avenue Henri-Matisse
06140 Vence
Tel.: +33 (0)4 93 58 03 26
The Maison Lacordaire, run by Dominican nuns, is located near the Matisse Chapel at the heart of a region rich in artistic and spiritual landmarks. The guest rooms occupy two renovated villas that overlook the city of Vence and the sea. Also available are courses in painting, working with stained-glass, etc.

VILLA ESTELLE

5, montée de la Bourgade
06800 Hauts-de-Cagnes
Tel.: +33 (0)4 92 02 89 83
(see pages 196–197)
This charming and historic old twelfth-century inn offers five distinctive guest rooms and one very comfortable suite, all decorated in warm colors. Errol Flynn, Orson Welles, and Modigliani are among those who once breakfasted on the vast terrace, which has an antique terra-cotta tile floor and a pergola with Italianate columns.

BOUCHES-DU-RHÔNE

LA BASTIDE / LE PIGEONNIER

Mas de Gouin
13310 Saint-Martin-de-Crau
Tel.: +33 (0)4 90 47 43 22
A farm estate with private gardens and individual swimming pools. Traditional Provençal cuisine is served by special order. Seasonal rentals are available.

CABANONS À LA MADRAGUE

7, chemin de la Madrague
13820 Ensuès-la-Redonne
Tel.: +33 (0)4 42 45 96 50
Overlooking a still somewhat wild seaside cove, this organization offers small apartments in fishermen's cottages for guests who love adventure and the outdoors. Families are welcome.

LA MAISON – DOMAINE DE BOURNISSAC

Montée d'Eyragues
13550 Paluds de Noves
Tel.: +33 (0)4 90 90 25 25
(see page 191)
This delightful hunting lodge overlooking the Alpine foothills and Ventoux and Luberon mountains was built in the fourteenth century for John XXII. Today it offers travelers a small number of inviting bedrooms and suites, plus a renowned restaurant featuring Mediterranean cuisine.

LE MAS DOU PASTRE

Quartier Sainte-Sixte
13810 Eygalières
Tel.: +33 (0)4 90 95 92 61
(see page 190)
This charming Provençal *mas* opposite a small chapel offers an authentic lifestyle in individually decorated bedrooms and a few gypsy caravans.

LA PAULINE

Chemin de la Fontaine-des-Tuiles
13100 Aix-en-Provence
Tel.: +33 (0)4 42 17 02 60
(see page 195)
An irresistible guest house paying homage to the charms of Pauline Borghèse, who used it as a love nest. Every bedroom has a private terrace with views over the vast seventeen-acre park that includes pools and fountains, a boxwood garden, statuary, and an

attractive swimming pool. Warm hospitality is provided by Linda Macquet.

LA PETITE MAISON

5, rue des Flots-Bleus
13007 Marseilles
Tel.: +33 (0)4 91 31 74 63
Less than thirty feet from the beaches, a guest house that seems like home. Cicada stencils indicate the bedroom numbers; two have sea views. The sea air stimulates guests' appetites for the fine table d'hôte meals.

LA QUINTA DES BAMBOUS

Chemin des Ribas
13100 Saint-Marc
Jaumegarde
Tel.: +33 (0)4 42 24 91 62
Contemporary Japanese-style structure on just under one acre of land, half of it natural forest, facing Mount Saint-Victoire. Two delightful guest rooms, the Lotus Room and the Peony (Pivoine) Room, open, respectively, onto an open patio planted with bamboo, and a garden filled with bamboo and lavender. A mirror water-lily pond lies just beyond the swimming pool.

RUE DU CHÂTEAU

24, rue du Château
13150 Tarascon
Tel.: +33 (0)4 90 91 09 99
In the old city, five Provençal-style guest rooms surround a central patio with red-ocher walls. Breakfast among the flowers is a special treat.

DRÔME

LE CLAIR DE PLUME

Place du Mail
26230 Grignan
Tel.: +33 (0)4 75 91 81 30
Fax: +33 (0)4 75 91 81 31
In a former convent near the rose-bush path and château made famous by Madame de Sévigné, the Clair de Plume offers ten lovely rooms in either Provençal or oriental style. Breakfast is served under a vine-covered trellis in the romantic garden.

GARD

LE MAS DE BARBUT

30220 Saint-Laurent d'Aygouze
Tel.: +33 (0)4 66 88 12 09
In the heart of Gard's Camargue region, this seventeenth-century sheep barn converted into a farmhouse offers three guest rooms decorated with a combination of Mexican and Provençal furniture. Gourmet meals and a warm welcome in a restful natural setting.

VAR

L'AUMÔNERIE

620, avenue de Font-Brun
83320 Carqueiranne
Tel.: +33 (0)4 94 58 53 56
A centuries-old former chaplain's residence and chapel shaded by ancient pines. Recently restored, the house's four guest rooms are furnished with family heirlooms. Very peaceful and hospitable.

LE CHÂTEAU DE SABLE

Avenue des Anthémis
83240 Cavalaire-sur-Mer
Tel.: +33 (0)4 94 00 45 90
Fax: +33 (0)4 94 64 05 34
France Ladouceur and her daughter, interior decorator Stéphanie Vatelot, have created a comfortable and stylish beach resort. Each of the five bedrooms—all decorated in a rustic-nautical style and with views of the sea—contains roomy beds, fashioned either in cast-iron by Astier de Villatte, or in the British antique-leather "Club" style.

DOMAINE DE MAJASTRE

Route de Moustiers
83630 Bauduen
Tel.: +33 (0)4 94 70 05 12
Famed truffle expert Philippe de Santis has opened his family home to guests. This manor, filled with antiques and surrounded by oak trees in the center of a 200-acre park, was once the residence of the Comtes de Blois. There are six bedrooms for the guests who, in summertime, enjoy sampling the chef's specialties, which are served in the garden by the swimming pool.

LE MAS DES GRAVIERS

Route des Rians
83910 Pourrières
Tel.: +33 (0)4 94 78 40 38
Amid the vineyards and lavender fields facing Mount Saint-Victoire, a typical eighteenth-century Provençal farmhouse, entirely restored by Andrea McGarvie-Munn. The two comfortable guest bedrooms and two suites are furnished with antiques—including settees, love-seats, and a kneading trough. Cooking courses and art exhibitions are also held here. Tours can be conducted in English, on request.

VAUCLUSE

L'ANASTASY

Île de la Bathelasse
84000 Avignon
Tel.: +33 (0)4 90 85 55 94
Fax: +33 (0)4 90 82 59 40
An old farmhouse typical of the Avignon region, offering five guest rooms. Olga Manguin's hospitality earns warm praise from theater buffs attending the drama festival—especially when she emerges from the kitchen bearing the Provençal and Italian specialties that have made her famous.

LA BASTIDE DE MARIE

84360 Ménerbes
Tel.: +33 (0)4 90 72 30 20
(see pages 174–175)
In the middle of a thirty-seven-acre vineyard, the quintessential Provençal lifestyle is distilled by Jocelyn Sibuet in the delightful rooms of her eighteenth-century farmhouse. Whether in the elegant indoor dining room or outdoors on the terrace, no one can resist the delectable specialties of the house.

BASTIDE LA COMBE

Chemin de Sainte-Croix
84110 Vaison-La-Romaine
Tel.: +33 (0)4 90 28 76 33
Not far from Vaison—a medieval Gallo-Roman city—this attractive farmhouse overlooking a vineyard-filled valley and surrounded by pine woods offers three double guest rooms and two suites. It also boasts fine reception rooms, a billiard room, library, and terraced gardens. The chef creates dazzling and imaginative seasonal menus based on the flavor and fragrance of the truffle.

CHAMBRES DE SÉJOUR AVEC VUE

84400 Saignon
Tel.: +33 (0)4 90 04 85 01
(see pages 192–193)
Nestled in the heart of a village perched on the slopes of the Luberon, this vividly and imaginatively decorated manor house provides a warm welcome to both its transient guests and its artists in residence.

LA CARRAIRE

84360 Lauris
Tel.: +33 (0)4 90 08 36 89
Fax: +33 (0)4 90 08 40 83
In the heart of the Luberon, Sophie Avon welcomes her guests in the main house of a seventeenth-century farm, which is reflected in the waters of an elegant irrigation basin. Relaxing hours around the pool, hiking in the Luberon park, French history, gourmet meals—in short, all the pleasures of Provence.

LA MAISON

84340 Beaumont-du-Ventoux
Tel.: +33 (0)4 90 65 15 50
Fax: +33 (0)4 90 65 23 29
This little eighteenth-century farmhouse surrounded by orchards is now an inviting inn. A happy gourmet clientele gathers for meals around tables set up under the linden trees. The three bedrooms decorated in the style and colors of Provence are highly prized by connoisseurs.

LA MAISON DES SOURCES

Chemin des Fraisses
84360 Lauris
Tel.: +33 (0)4 90 08 22 19
This *mas* surrounded by greenery offers four spectacular bedrooms accommodating two, three, or four guests (in the "nun's" room). All of them have private baths or showers, and an

unobstructed view of the Provençal countryside. There is no extra charge for the lulling hum of the cicadas.

LA RIBAUDE
84110 Le Crestet
Tel.: +33 (0)4 90 36 36 11
Near Vaison-la-Romaine, this guest house— superbly decorated by owner Renata Luhmann—invites travelers to explore the steep little streets of a village that was once the fief of the bishops of Vaison. The ravishing antique furniture in each differently colored suite is a tribute to Provence. The patio, flowered terraces, and swimming pool overlooking Mount Ventoux make this highly popular in summertime.

LE CASTELAS
84400 Sivergues
Tel.: +33 (0)4 90 74 60 89
(see pages 174, 188–189)
On the virgin slopes of the Luberon, a fortified farmhouse that was once a sheep barn offers an authentic sense of novelty in slightly rustic but charming guest rooms. Dormitory for children. A convivial atmosphere is sustained by the indomitable personality of Gianni the shepherd.

LE JAS DE MONSIEUR
84240 Grambois
Tel.: +33 (0)4 90 77 92 08
(see page 194)

Standing on a vast 320-acre estate in the midst of a typically Provençal landscape, this eighteenth-century manor house offers three guest rooms. The swimming pool and park are open to guests.

LES GRANGES DU BOSQUET
1473, chemin du Bosquet
84800 L'Isle-sur-la-Sorgue
Tel.: +33 (0)4 90 21 19 89
An original guest-house formula: ten bedrooms decorated extremely tastefully, spread throughout the various houses and old stable composing a little hamlet. The rooms are separated from one another by village courtyards. A magical, inspiring spot.

LE MAS DE LA BEAUME
84220 Gordes
Tel.: +33 (0)4 90 72 02 96
Not far from Gordes, this lovely stone farmhouse with a view of the church and château has preserved the essential soul of the Luberon within its walls. Children are delighted by the caravan in the garden. Irresistibly tempting breakfasts prepared by Nadine Camus.

LE MAS DES FALAISES
84210 Le Beaucet
Tel.: +33 (0)4 90 74 15 71
A fine stone manor house standing on two-and-a-half acres of terraced land

in a luxuriant landscape facing superb cliffs. A cool dip in the pool after a hike through the surrounding countryside is a real pleasure. Six bedrooms accommodate twelve guests. The owners, who live on another part of the estate, are happy to advise on local hiking itineraries.

LE MAS DES SONGES
1631, chemin du Pérussier
84170 Monteux
Tel.: +33 (0)4 90 65 49 20
This old sheep barn overlooking the Vaison plain offers spacious bedrooms, two of them duplexes. The setting is refined and contemporary. Touches of color on pale concrete set the decorative tone. Breakfast is served outside under a shady arbor.

LE MOURRE
84580 Oppède-le-Vieux
Tel.: +33 (0)4 90 76 99 31
Attractive guest rooms have been installed in an old dovecote, a flour mill, and a fine farmhouse, on land shaded by fig trees and surrounded by vines.

LE SILENCE DES ANGES
Quartier Pérussol
84180 Oppède-le-Vieux
Tel.: +33 (0)4 90 76 86 63
Standing on thirty acres of land overlooking the Luberon valley, Le Silence des Anges affords exceptional views of

Mount Vaucluse and Mount Ventoux. Four spacious and comfortable bedrooms are decorated with a medley of objects in a contemporary spirit.

VILLA SAINT-LOUIS
35, rue Henri-de-Savournin
84160 Lourmarin
Tel.: +33 (0)4 90 68 39 18
(see pages 198–200)
This secular domain was adroitly transformed by Michel Lassallette, the late interior decorator of unerring taste, who loved furnishing old residences by combining different historical periods. The exceptionally warm hospitality of his wife, Bernadette, and the enthusiasm of their daughter, Mapie, continue to make this place a particularly appealing one.

GARDENS

Passionately tended and protected, these exceptional sites are the crown jewels of France's South. They have much to teach us through their lyrical beauty: they offer a permanent spectacle, where tamed nature is designed to stimulate reverie.

ALPES-DE-HAUTE-PROVENCE

LE PRIEURÉ DE SALAGON
04300 Mane

Tel.: +33 (0)4 92 75 70 70
This garden, planned to reflect the ethno-botanical heritage of Haute Provence, is a living record of useful plants. Installed at the foot of a ravishing medieval priory, the garden-archive of medicinal herbs now has a rival: the modern-day garden.

ALPES-MARITIMES

LE CLOS DU PEYRONNET
Avenue Aristide-Briand
06500 Menton
Tel.: +33 (0)4 93 35 72 15
(see page 16)
In Menton, not far from the frontier with Italy, William Waterfield perpetuates a family tradition of making exotic gardens with his terraced creation containing rare species and a spectacular water-stair that runs along the Mediterranean Sea.

FONDATION MAEGHT
06570 Saint-Paul-de-Vence
Tel.: +33 (0)4 93 32 81 63
In the garden-showcase surrounding this famed museum of modern art, sculptures by the greatest masters of the twentieth century line a pathway that leads to the Giacometti courtyard and the Miró maze. The fountain is by Pol Bury, mural mosaics by Tal Coat, and the pool by Georges Braque.

JARDIN DU MONASTÈRE
Place du Monastère de Cimiez
06000 Nice
Tel.: +33 (0)4 97 13 20 00
In this garden with a medieval flavor, old pergolas covered with climbing roses and a lawn dotted with sweet and bitter orange and tangerine trees unite to form an extremely harmonious whole.

LA SERRE DE LA MADONE
74, route de Gorbio
06500 Menton
Tel.: +33 (0)4 93 57 73 90
(see pages 45, 50–53)
First planted in 1920 by Lawrence Johnston, who landscaped Hidcote Manor in England, this garden—which is currently in the process of being restored— contains numerous enclosed spaces serving as theme gardens: water, shade, and light gardens; gardens devoted to a single plant. From top to bottom of the terraces, micro-climates accommodate a wide variety of species. Each season has its respective blooms. The old-fashioned greenhouse is a rarity.

LES COLOMBIÈRES
Boulevard Garavan
06500 Menton
Tel.: +33 (0)4 92 10 97 10
(see page 16)
This property, designed at the beginning of the twentieth century by the

RENTAL PROPERTIES

LUBERON INVESTISSEMENT
La Combe
84220 Gordes
Tel.: +33 (0)4 90 72 07 55
Vincent Bœuf and his team efficiently and courteously find the most charming Provençal *mas* and *bastides* available for rent during the summer. The agency has a select list of holiday rental properties in the Luberon, the Alpine foothills, and the Aix region.

LOCATIONS À LA SEMAINE : MICHÈLE ET BRUNO VIARD.
Tel.: 04 91 22 11 98
(see pages 122–127)
A farmhouse at the foot of the Luberon (occupancy 6–7) and a little country cabin (occupancy 2–3). Both properties include swimming pool.

application to the Menton Heritage Service.

LE PALAIS CARNOLÈS
Avenue de la Madone
06500 Menton
Tel.: +33 (0)4 93 35 49 71
A two-and-a-half-acre public park filled with majestic palms and some fifty varieties of citrus tree. The museum, which was formerly the summer residence of the Grimaldi family, contains a fine collection of eighteenth-century paintings.

LE VAL RAMEH
Avenue Saint-Jacques
06500 Menton
Tel.: +33 (0)4 93 35 86 72
The variety of its species, arrangement of its displays, and diversity of its reconstituted environments give this botanical garden a unique atmosphere. Don't miss the extensive collection of exotic edible fruits.

VILLA DOMERGUE
15, impasse Fiesole
06400 Cannes
Tel.: +33 (0)4 93 68 91 92
This building, owned by the municipality of Cannes, was designed by Jean-Gabriel Domergue. It overlooks splendid formal Italian gardens ornamented with basins and statuary. Don't miss the majestic Florentine-style staircase affording an impressive view over the Bay of Cannes. Tours by appointment.

LA VILLA EILEN-ROC
Avenue de Beaumont
06600 Antibes
Tel.: +33 (0)4 93 67 74 33
This rocky promontory on the Cap d'Antibes has been transformed into a vast twenty-seven-acre wooded park serving as a showcase for the villa built by Charles Garnier, and today owned by the city of Antibes. Suspended above the sea, this still somewhat wild but charming Mediterranean garden is open to the public two days a week, on Tuesdays and Wednesdays. On Wednesdays, visitors can also visit the upper floor of the villa.

BOUCHES-DU-RHÔNE

LE JARDIN DE L'ALCHIMISTE
Mas de la Brune
13810 Eygalières
Tel.: +33 (0)4 90 90 67 77
Designed by landscape architects Arnaud Maurières and Eric Ossart, who are also responsible for the medieval garden at the Cluny Museum in Paris, the Alchemist's garden illustrates the Great Work—which is the ultimate goal of alchemy—through imaginative expressions of the two partners' familiarity with the plants, thematic symbols, mystic numbers, and colors of this arcane science.

COOKING COURSES

L'ÉCOLE DE CUISINE DU SOLEIL L'AMANDIER
06250 Mougins
Tel. : 04 93 75 35 70
This cooking school, founded by Roger Vergé, is aimed at amateur cooks; one week per month they are tutored by skilled chef Serge Chollet. Courses are conducted in English and French.

PATRICIA WELLS
Chemin des Fontaines
84110 Vaison-la-Romaine

e-mail : cookingclass@patriciawells.com
(see pages 14–17)
Patricia Wells, ambassador of Provençal cuisine in the United States and renowned cookbook author, conducts a five-day (Sunday evening through Friday) cooking course several times a year in the privacy of her Vaison-la-Romaine farmhouse. The courses are theme-based, and include tastings and tours of local markets. Recipes feature seasonal vegetables and herbs, and meals are accompanied

(appropriately) by a Clos Chanteduc, the wine produced on Wells's estate. Groups of ten (maximum); courses are conducted in English only.

MAS DES GRAVIERS
Route des Rians
83910 Pourrières
Tel. : 04 94 78 40 38
In her lovely farmhouse at the foot of Mount Sainte-Victoire, Andrea McGarvie-Munn offers cooking courses in the autumn. Courses conducted in English and French.

famed landscape architect Ferdinand Bac, offers a space punctuated with fountains and sculptures reflecting Mediterranean culture. A fifteen-acre delight, the garden has admirable views of the Garavan bay and the old village of Menton. It is private, but open to the public from July 1st through August 6th, by reservation only, on

JARDINS D'ALBERTAS
R.N. 8
13320 Bouc-Bel-Air
Tel.: +33 (0)4 42 22 29 77
(see pages 45, 54–57)
Now a listed historic monument, these gardens were designed in 1751, and show a keen awareness of both terrain and architecture. A blend of French and Italian influences, the gardens have fountains, pools, and statuary, boxwood, yew and evergreen oak: all combine to transform them into dramatic theaters of perspective.

PAVILLON VENDÔME
32, rue Célony
13100 Aix-en-Provence

Tel.: +33 (0)4 42 21 05 78
Surrounded by a park laid out in the formal French style, the Pavillon Vendôme's setting and interior decoration are typical of an eighteenth-century Aix manor house. The façade, to which an upper floor was added in the seventeenth century, is lined with Ionic, Doric, and Corinthian columns.

VAR

DOMAINE DU RAYOL
Avenue du Commandant-Rigaud
83820 Le Rayol-Canadel
Tel.: +33 (0)4 98 04 44 00
(see pages 38–39)
Landscape architect Gilles Clément has chosen to

display flora native to regions of the world with a Mediterranean climate. Creating natural environments on the site, he draws his inspiration from the Mediterranean basin, southeastern California, central Chile, the Cape region in South Africa, and southern Australia.

VILLA NOAILLES
Parc Saint-Bernard
Montée de Noailles
83260 Hyères
Tel.: +33 (0)4 94 35 90 65
Designed by Robert Mallet-Stevens in 1920 for the Vicomte de Noailles, this terraced garden combines Mediterranean and subtropical species.

Located below the famed Villa de Noailles, it affords a superb view of the bay and its islands. Of special note is the cubist garden, planted with succulent species, designed by Guevrekian.

GARDEN TOURS

SERENOA CONSEIL
9, boulevard de Rothschild
06130 Grasse
Tel.: +33 (0)4 93 36 58 04
Small-group tours of magnificent private gardens. A picnic lunch is included in the price. It is a good idea to reserve your place well in advance, since registration closes two weeks prior to the tour date.

VINEYARDS

The vineyards listed below are well worth a visit. Visitors will be fascinated by their history and the beauty of their settings, and can also take advantage of the opportunity to purchase excellent wines produced according to traditional methods.

ALPES-MARITIMES

CHÂTEAU DE BELLET
440, chemin de Saquier
06200 Nice
Tel.: +33 (0)4 93 37 81 57

The slopes around Nice produce excellent vintages, including those of Bellet (*Appellation d'Origine Contrôlée*). The Château de Bellet vintage is one of the best. Available for sale on the estate, by appointment.

BOUCHES-DU-RHÔNE

CHÂTEAU DALMERAN
41–43 Chemin Romain
13103 Saint-Étienne-du-Grès
Tel.: +33 (0)4 90 49 04 04
Discovered by enterprising connoisseurs, the red, rosé, and white wines produced on this magnificent estate are currently served in some of the finest restaurants in the world.

CHÂTEAU DE LA GALINIÈRE
13790 Châteauneuf-le-Rouge
Tel.: +33 (0)4 42 29 09 84
This long-established 200-acre vineyard at the foot of Mount Saint-Victoire was restored in 1997 by Amédée Laurent Musso, an antiques dealer based in Aix and Paris, and two œnologists. Tours of the magnificent cellar with its modern equipment also provide visitors with an opportunity to stock up on Côtes-de-Provence and Côtes-du-Rhône wines.

CHÂTEAU DE LA GAUDE
Route des Pinchinats
13100 Aix-en-Provence

Tel.: +33 (0)4 42 21 64 19
A vineyard producing Côteaux d'Aix-en-Provence (*Appellation d'Origine Contrôlée*) wines. The La Gaude vineyard covers some fifty acres on the hilly slopes used by Yves Robert as the setting for his film based on Marcel Pagnol's book *Le Château de ma mère* ("My Mother's Castle"). The vines planted around the summit of Le Capéou have been tended according to traditional methods for at least thirty years, amply confirming the vineyard's excellent potential.

CHÂTEAU SIMONE
13590 Meyreuil
Tel.: +33 (0)4 42 66 92 58
This ravishingly lovely Renaissance château in a formal French park is renowned for the quality of its marvelous red and rosé wines, and for their history—they were once enjoyed by Le Roi René, who was Duke of Anjou, Count of Provence and Piedmont. Tours can be made by appointment.

VAR

CHÂTEAU SAINTE-ROSELINE
83460 Les-Arcs-sur-Argens
Tel.: +33 (0)4 94 99 50 30
One of the nineteen official AOC (*Appellation d'Origine Contrôlée*) Côtes-de-Provence vintages. The Château Sainte-Roseline

has been a historic landmark ever since the fourteenth century, and it still produces some of the very best Côtes-de-Provence wines. Of special note is the "Lampe-de-Méduse," developed by the estate in 1950.

DOMAINE GAVOTY
Le Grand-Campdumy
83340 Cabasse
Tel.: +33 (0)4 94 69 72 39
Planted on land rich in chalk and clay, this 130-acre vineyard proudly displays its official Côtes-de-Provence listing and produces red wines that age well.

VAUCLUSE

CHÂTEAU LA CANORGUE
Route du Pont-Julien
84480 Bonnieux
Tel.: +33 (0)4 90 75 81 01
A small traditional family vineyard using several root stocks. The wines, aged in oak casks and estate-bottled, have frequently been awarded gold medals at agricultural fairs in Paris, Macon, Blayais, Avignon, and Orange.

CHÂTEAU UNANG
Route de Méthamis
84570 Malemort-du-Comtat
Tel.: +33 (0)4 90 69 91 37
This château at the foot of Mount Ventoux, restored during the eighteenth century, is one of the oldest in the Vaucluse. The château itself is not

open to the public, but its splendid grounds are worth a visit—a trip that can be combined, of course, with the purchase of some wine.

CHÂTEAU DE LA NERTHE
Route de Sorgues
84230 Châteauneuf-du-Pape
This wine, the highest-ranked Châteauneuf-du-Pape, is stored in vaulted sixteenth-century wine cellars. New wine, pressed from thirteen different varieties of grape, is allowed to age in the cellar's 350 casks. Bottled vintages, some of which are reserved for fine restaurants, are placed in huge racks.

CHÂTEAU LA VERRERIE
Route de Cavaillon
84160 Lourmarin
This seventy-five-acre vineyard—where the Descours family shows respect for both soil and root stock—stands below the nineteenth-century annex to a ruined fifteenth-century building that was once a glassworks belonging to the Comtes de Provence. The wines are notable for their complexity and their aging qualities.

CHÂTEAU VAL JOANIS
Chemin de Val Joanis
84120 Pertuis
Tel.: +33 (0)4 90 79 20 77

(see pages 44–49)
One of the few French wine-growing estates that has existed unchanged over the centuries. Today, the Château Val Joanis estate's hospitality service offers tours of the cellars and gardens, plus wine and olive-oil tastings.

CHÂTEAU DE MILLE
Quartier Mille
84440 Apt
Tel.: +33 (0)4 90 74 11 94
(see pages 142–145)
This château, once the summer residence of Pope Clément V, is an architectural gem. It is also one of the oldest wine-producing estates in the Luberon. Its wines are fine quality and tannic. Oak casks fill the extremely modern cellar.

DOMAINE DE LA CITADELLE
84560 Ménerbes
Tel.: +33 (0)4 90 72 41 58
On the slopes of the Luberon, Yves Rousset-Rouard has created a 100-acre estate where grapevines are cultivated according to traditional methods. La Citadelle also boasts a picturesque Museum of Corkscrews.

DOMAINE DE LA ROYÈRE
84500 Oppède
Tel.: +33 (0)4 90 76 87 76
Facing Oppède-le-Vieux at the foot of the Luberon, the vineyards of the Domaine de la

Royère produce superb, prize-winning Côtes du Luberon and Côtes du Ventoux vintages. The owner-vintners, Anne and Jean-Pierre Hugues, also have a well-equipped distillery for the production, according to traditional methods, of renowned brandies made from grape marc and fruit—notably plum, cherry, pear, and melon. Lavender honey is another specialty of the house.

MUSEUMS

Selected for the quality of their collections illustrating life in Provence, these cultural institutions offer an exciting journey of discovery through the wealth and elegance of traditional arts and crafts in the South of France.

ALPES-DE-HAUTE-PROVENCE

LE MUSÉE DE LA FAÏENCE
Place du Presbytère
04360 Moustiers-Sainte-Marie
Tel.: +33 (0)4 92 74 61 64
Examples of historic Clérissy-blue faïence, plus some more contemporary items.

ALPES-MARITIMES

GALERIE BEAUBOURG
Château Notre-Dame-des-Fleurs
06140 Vence
Tel.: +33 (0)4 93 24 52 00
In the terraced park surrounding a farmhouse converted into a gallery of modern art, Pierre and Marianne Nahon have added a sculpture garden featuring works by major contemporary artists, including Arman, Tinguely, Louis Cane, and Niki de Saint-Phalle.

CHÂTEAU DE LA NAPOULE
Association d'Art de La Napoule
06210 La Napoule
Tel.: +33 (0)4 93 49 95 05
(see pages 137, 159)
A medieval dreamworld created in the early twentieth century by an eccentric American couple: Henry Clews, a sculptor; and his wife Mary, a landscape architect.

MUSÉE FRAGONARD
20, boulevard Fragonard
06130 Grasse
Tel.: +33 (0)4 93 36 44 65
(see pages 165–166)
Collections of perfume-related items spanning 3,000 years displayed in a traditionally furnished town house. Guided tours explaining classic methods of manufacture. Fragonard fragrances and toiletries available for sale.

MUSÉE INTERNATIONAL DE LA PARFUMERIE
8, place du Cours-Honoré-Cresp
06130 Grasse
Tel.: +33 (0)4 93 36 80 20
A museum dedicated to the history of perfumery and the development of perfume technology over the centuries. An amazing collection of bottles and objects related to the art of perfumery from ancient times to the present.

MUSÉE PROVENÇAL DU COSTUME ET DU BIJOU
2, rue Jean-Ossola
06130 Grasse
Tel.: +33 (0)4 93 36 44 65
(see pages 166–167)
In a town house once owned by Mirabeau's sister, the Marquise de Clapier-Cabris, Hélène Costa has assembled a collection of antique clothing and jewelry reflecting the lives of local aristocrats, artisans, and peasants.

MUSÉE MASSÉNA
65, rue de France
06000 Nice
Tel.: +33 (0)4 93 88 11 34
A collection of furniture from Provence and Nice; faïence made in Marseilles, Apt, and Moustiers, and fine examples of work by painters native to Nice.

PALAIS LASCARIS
15, rue Droite
06300 Nice
Tel.: +33 (0)4 93 62 72 40
This residence, which earned its historic-monument listing in 1946, displays items typical of both aristocratic and peasant lifestyles in the Nice region. Fine furniture and an extensive collection of Genoese baroque art. One gallery entirely devoted to traditional folk art from the area.

PRIEURÉ DU VIEUX LOGIS
59, avenue Saint-Barthélemy
06000 Nice
Tel.: +33 (0)4 93 62 72 40
A collection of medieval and Renaissance sacred art, practical objects, and furniture (sixteenth and seventeenth century).

MUSÉE DE LA POTERIE
Rue Sicard
06600 Vallauris
Tel.: +33 (0)4 93 64 66 51
Housing a replica of an early twentieth-century pottery workshop. Also, an impressive collection of antique faïence from the foremost workshops in Marseilles, as well as Provençal ceramics from the late seventeenth through the nineteenth centuries.

MUSÉE RENOIR
Chemin des Collettes
06800 Cagnes-sur-Mer
Tel.: +33 (0)4 93 20 61 07
This large estate was purchased in 1907 by the artists Pierre-Auguste Renoir, in order to save its olive groves from imminent destruction. Renoir spent the last twelve years of his life here. The house has been preserved just as it was when he occupied it, and contains a splendid collection.

VILLA EPHRUSSI DE ROTHSCHILD
06290 Saint-Jean-Cap-Ferrat
Tel.: +33 (0)4 93 01 33 09
(see pages 154–157)
Surrounded by the seven magnificent theme-based gardens installed by the Baroness Ephrussi de Rothschild—who drew on what she saw during her travels around the world for their design—the museum displays over 5,000 art works and an impressive collection of furnishings, objets d'art, lamps, tapestries, etc.

VILLA KÉRYLOS
7, rue Gustave-Eiffel
06310 Beaulieu-sur-Mer
Tel.: +33 (0)4 93 01 61 70
(see pages 10–11, 158–161)
The Villa Kérylos, located between Nice and Monaco, is a listed historical monument. Designed to replicate as closely as possible the ancient Greek villas of the Periclean Age, it has no equal anywhere in the world. Its frescoes and mosaics, furniture and objets d'art all contribute to the authentically Grecian mood.

BOUCHES-DU-RHÔNE

ATELIER PAUL CÉZANNE
9, avenue Paul-Cézanne
13100 Aix-en-Provence
Tel.: +33 (0)4 42 21 06 53
In 1901 Paul Cézanne purchased a plot of land on the Lauves hill and built a studio in which to paint. According to Cézanne, it was the place of creation of a "new art;" he proclaimed himself the first practitioner of this art. In fine weather Cézanne moved his easel into the open, facing Mount Sainte-Victoire. Dozens of paintings, now held by the greatest museums in the world—including *Les Baigneuses* ("The Bathers") and numerous views of Mount Sainte-Victoire—were executed in this hushed and sunlit studio.

HÔTEL D'OLIVARY
Rue du Quatre-Septembre
13100 Aix-en-Provence
Tel.: +33 (0)4 42 26 86 01
Designed by Jean Daret, this seventeenth-century town house off the Place de Quatre-Dauphins contains a series of three salons attractively decorated with pier glass and carved moldings. The formal French garden with its boxwood-lined alleys, tall trees, and chalice-fountain pool is an additional attraction. Reservations for guided tours must be made in advance by telephone.

MUSÉE DU VIEIL AIX
17, rue Gaston-Saporta
13100 Aix-en-Provence

Tel.: +33 (0)4 42 21 43 55
A collection of furniture
and faïence displayed in a
fine seventeenth-century
town house.

MUSEON
ARLATEN
29, rue de la République
13200 Arles
Tel.: +33 (0)4 90 93 58 11
Bread boxes, kneading
troughs—all the utensils
typically found in a
Provençal farmhouse—are
displayed at this attractive
museum in the heart of
the old city.

MUSÉE CHARLES
DÉMERY-
SOULEIADO
39, rue Proudhon
13150 Tarascon
Tel.: +33 (0)4 90 91 08 80
This delightful museum,
named after the founder of
the fabric company,
Souleiado, and based in the
Souleiado town house,
traces the history of fabric
printing in Provence since
the seventeenth century.
Collections of costumes,
antique quilted fabrics,
sacred and folk objects, and
fine mixed-clay faïence.

MUSÉE DE LA
FAÏENCE
Château Pastré
155, avenue de Montredon
13008 Marseilles
Tel.: +33 (0)4 91 72 43 47
In this building, set
within a fine park
bordered by hills and sea,
are extraordinary displays
of antique Marseilles
and Provençal faïence,

dating from the late
seventeenth through the
nineteenth century.

MUSÉE DES ARTS
ET TRADITIONS
POPULAIRES DU
CHÂTEAU GOMBERT
5, place des Héros
13013 Marseilles
Tel.: +33 (0)4 91 68 14 38
Extensive, interesting
collections of Provençal
folk art, including
costumes and furniture.

MUSÉE GROBERT-
LABADIÉ
140, boulevard Longchamp
13001 Marseilles
Tel.: +33 (0)4 91 62 21 82
The original decor of this
town house has been
preserved, and today
serves as the backdrop for
a fine collection of
furniture and faïence.

GARD

LE MUSÉE DE LA
POTERIE
MÉDITERRANÉENNE
Rue de la Fontaine
30700 Saint-Quentin-de-
la-Poterie
Tel.: +33 (0)4 66 03 65 86
In this display area within
the Maison de la Terre, 250
ceramic household items
trace the traditional daily
life of peasants living
around the Mediterranean.

VAR

MUSÉE DES ARTS
ET TRADITIONS
POPULAIRES
15, rue Roumanille

83300 Draguignan
Tel.: +33 (0)4 94 47 05 72
Collections illustrating
daily life in Provence. Of
special note is the fine
old-fashioned kitchen.

CHÂTEAUX
AND BASTIDES

*Tours that offer a unique
opportunity to learn about
château life, at historic sites
that often possess marvelous
gardens as well.*

**ALPES-DE-HAUTE-
PROVENCE**

CHÂTEAU DE
SAUVAN
04300 Mane
Tel.: +33 (0)4 92 75 05 64
(see page 8)
This ravishing Regency
château, surrounded by a
garden laid out in the
formal French style, is
open to the public two
afternoons per week,
on Thursdays and on
Sundays. The owners
of the château, who are
both connoisseurs of
eighteenth-century
furniture and painting,
have recently restored
their home in the elegant
and frivolous spirit of its
period. Group tours are
by appointment. Lunch is
available on request.

BOUCHES-DU-RHÔNE

CHÂTEAU DE
BARBENTANE
1, rue du Château
13570 Barbentane

Tel.: +33 (0)4 90 95 51 07
(see page 137)
The Marquis de
Barbentane's residence,
dubbed the "*Petit Trianon
du Soleil*" and described as
"the most Italian of all
Provence châteaux," has
been spared by history.
Built in the second half of
the seventeenth century
by architect Louis-
François de la Valfenière,
this listed historical
monument has retained all
the charm of a pleasure-
palace inhabited without
interruption for centuries.
The carved moldings and
Carrara-marble marquetry
flooring, installed by
Joseph-Pierre Balthazar
de Puget, Marquis of
Barbentane and Louis
XV's ambassador to
Florence, combine the
refinement of Tuscan
villas with the majestic
elegance characteristic of
Île-de-France châteaux.
As visitors stroll through
the salons and descend the
ornamental staircase, they
can explore eighteenth-
century Provençal art
through objets d'art,
statues, Aubusson
tapestries, faïence, and
period Louis XV and
Louis XVI furnishings.

LA MIGNARDE
Les Pinchinats
13100 Aix-en-Provence
Tel.: +33 (0)4 42 96 41 86
Once the summer
residence of Pauline
Borghèse, who was
Napoleon Bonaparte's
younger sister. The house

is surrounded by an
eighteenth-century
formal French garden
designed by Nicolas
Ledoux. Fine statuary
and a mirror pool.

PAVILLON
VENDÔME
32, rue Célony
13100 Aix-en-Provence
Tel.: +33 (0)4 42 21 05 78
This building, erected in
the seventeenth century
for the Duc de Vendôme,
was given an additional
story during the following
century. The interior
contains an extensive
collection of furniture,
paintings, sculptures, and
objets d'art that illustrate
the highly aristocratic
lifestyle once prevalent in
the Aix region.

DRÔME

CHÂTEAU DE
GRIGNAN
26230 Grignan
Tel.: +33 (0)4 75 46 51 56
(see page 137)
A fine example of the
architecture prevalent in
southeastern France.
Formerly the residence of
Françoise de Grignan,
beloved daughter of
Madame la Marquise de
Sévigné. This Renaissance
château was made famous
by the fascinating series
of letters written by the
marquise to her daughter.
The marquise died here.

CHÂTEAU DE
SUZE-LA-ROUSSE
26790 Suze-la-Rousse

Standing in the heart of
the Rhône Valley
vineyards, the Château de
Suze-la-Rousse—which
today houses the
University of Wine—
presents a stunning
contrast between military
and civilian architecture.
Courses in œnology are
available to professionals
and amateurs.

VAUCLUSE

CHÂTEAU
D'ANSOUIS
84240 Ansouis
Tel.: +33 (0)4 90 09 82 70
(see pages 45, 137)
Still inhabited today by
the Duc and Duchesse de
Sabran, this château and
its garden illustrate the
charm and refinement
typical of great Provençal
residences. Behind the
château's austere façade lie
a series of salons that are
adorned with Flemish
tapestries and antique
Italian and French
furniture. The kitchen,
with its eighteenth-
century Provençal
furnishings and vast
fireplace, is both warm
and spectacular—as is the
sixteenth-century staircase
with its coffered ceiling.

CHÂTEAU DE
LOURMARIN
84160 Lourmarin
Tel.: +33 (0)4 90 68 15 23
Against a lovely
background of painted
wood, visitors can admire
the magnificently
furnished apartments.

A TOUR OF THE ISLANDS

LÉRINS ISLANDS

The Lérins islands of Sainte Marguerite and Saint Honorat, a short boat-ride from the Cannes Croisette, are ideal for memorable excursions along the shore of the Alpes-Maritimes.

SAINTE MARGUERITE ISLAND

The luxuriant nature-trail winding through this idyllic site allows visitors to identify a wide range of plants: every species of pine and eucalyptus, cedars, and magnificent underbrush composed of heather, arbutus, and mastic. Of special note: the fortified castle in which the Man in the Iron Mask was imprisoned.

SAINT HONORAT ISLAND

On their estate surrounding a fortified monastery, monks belonging to the Cistercian Sénanque Order cultivate grapes, rosemary, and lavender. They also produce a liqueur made from forty-four plants, and a dry wine called La Vendange-des-Moines. The island's many natural treasures include lotus trees, magnolias, Judas trees, Aleppo pines, cypress, and eucalyptus.

LEVANT ISLANDS

PORT-CROS AND PORQUEROLLES ISLANDS

These two islands, Port-Cros and Porquerolles, are still relatively unspoilt by crowds or construction work. They can be reached by boat from Giens, Toulon, Lavandou, and Cavalaire. The best way to tour Porquerolles is by bicycle—pedaling to the lighthouse while breathing in the scent of paths bordered with pine, heather, and myrtle; and exploring the beautiful and fairly deserted beaches. A listed national parkland, the Island of Port-Cros is perfect for walking tours. Visitors on foot can study each magical site in detail, and enjoy the Route des Crêtes, where gaps in the eucalyptus and pine woods afford stunning views of the Mediterranean Sea.

FRENCH LANGUAGE COURSES IN PROVENCE

The following organizations offer people of all levels a chance to study French while in Provence. Short- or longer-term courses are available.

INSTITUT D'ENSEIGNEMENT DE LA LANGUE FRANÇAISE SUR LA CÔTE D'AZUR
66, avenue de Toulon
83400 Hyères
Tel.: +33 (0)4 94 65 03 31
Fax: +33 (0)4 94 65 81 22
www.elfca.com

SOUFFLE
9, cours des Arts-et-Métiers
13100 Aix-en-Provence
Tel.: +33 (0)4 42 93 47 90
info@is-aix.com
www.is-aix.com

CREA-LANGUES
La Monastère de Ségriès
04260 Mousiters Sainte Marie
Tel.: +33 (0)4 92 77 74 58
info@crealangues.com

TOURIST INFORMATION

These offices are run by the French government for potential visitors to Provence.

UNITED STATES

PROVENCE-ALPES-CÔTE D'AZUR REGIONAL TOURIST BOARD
Michael Darthiail
444 Madison Avenue
16th Floor
New York, NY 10022
Tel./Fax: (212) 838-7855
mardthiail@francetourism.com

MAISON DE LA FRANCE
676 North Michigan Ave.
Chicago, IL 60611
Tel.: (312) 751-7800
Fax: (312) 337-6339

MAISON DE LA FRANCE
9151 Wilshire Blvd.
Suite 715
Beverly Hill, CA 90212
Tel.:(310) 271-6665
Fax: (310) 276-2835
fgto@gte.net

MAISON DE LA FRANCE
1 Biscayne Tower
Suite 1750
2 South Biscayne Blvd.
Miami, FL 33131
Tel.: (305) 373-8177
Fax: (305) 373-5828

UNITED KINGDOM

MAISON DE LA FRANCE
178 Piccadilly
London W1 9AL
Tel.: 020 6824 4123
Fax: 020 7493 6594
www.franceguide.com

AUSTRALIA

MAISON DE LA FRANCE
Level 20, 25 Bligh Street
Sydney
NSW 2000
Tel.: (61) 02 9231 5244
Fax: (61) 02 9221 8682
france@bigpond.net.au

CANADA

MAISON DE LA FRANCE
1981 Ave.
McGill College
Suite 490
Montreal
QUE H3A 2W9
Tel.: (514) 876-9881
Fax: (514) 845-4868
mfrance@attcanada.net

RESTAURANTS ABROAD

UNITED STATES

PASTIS
9 Ninth Avenue
at Little W. 12th Street
New York, NY 10014
Tel.: (212) 929-4844

PROVENCE CAFÉ
1518 Montana Avenue
Santa Monica, CA 90403
Tel.:(310) 656-6880

TWIN PALMS
101 West Garden Street
Los Angeles, CA 91105
Tel.: (626) 577-2567

UNITED KINGDOM

BISTRO DANIEL
26 Sussex Place
London
W2 2TH
Tel.: (020) 7262 6073

AUSTRALIA

LE BOULEVARD
40 Avalon Parade
Avalon
Sydney, NSW 2107
Tel.: (02) 9918-8933

CAFÉ DE MARIE
166 Victoria Street
Potts Point
Sydney, NSW 2011
Tel.: (02) 9331-3732

CAFÉ SEL ET POIVRE
263 Victoria Street
Darlinghurst
Sydney, NSW 2010
Tel.: (02) 9361-6530
Fax: (02) 9360-8926

PROVENÇAL GOODS ABROAD

UNITED STATES

LA MAISON MODERNE
144 West 19th Street
New York, NY 10011
Tel.: (212) 691-9603

ROMANCING PROVENCE LIMITED
225 Fifth Avenue
New York, NY 10010
Tel.: (212) 481-9879

SAVON
25 Christopher Street
New York, NY 10014
Tel.: (212) 463-7637

LA PROVENCE
239 Chartres Street
New Orleans, LA 70130
Tel: (504) 299-0772
Fax: (504) 299-0773
www.provencelinens.com

LES INDIENNES DE NÎMES
U.S. Agent: M. Vacherie
Tel.: (404) 816-7825

SOLEIL EN PROVENCE

402 Washington Street
Wellesly, MA 02482
Tel.: (781) 239-1101
www.provence-shop.com

FRENCH COUNTRY
ANTIQUES
1000 King Street

Alexandria, VA 22314
Tel.: (703) 548-8563

BELLE PROVENCE
P.O. Box 2854
Rohnert Park, CA
94927
www.belle-provence.com

UNITED KINGDOM

LP ANTIQUES
The Old Brewery
Short Acre Street
Walsall
West Midlands
England

Tel.: +44 (0)1922 746 764
Fax: +44 (0)1922 611 316

LES OLIVADES
Mail order only.
Tel.: +44 (0)207 731 0444
Fax: +44 (0)207 731 0788
www.les-olivades.com

CANADA

EN PROVENCE INC.

PUGH'S ANTIQUES
Tel.: +44 (0)1404 42860
www.pughes-antiques-
export.com

20 Hazelton Ave.
Toronto, Ontario
Tel.: (1) 416-975-9400

L'ESPRIT DE
PROVENCE
www.lespritprovence.com

BIBLIOGRAPHY

FLAMMARION TITLES

Biehn, Michel. *Recipes from a Provençal Kitchen*. Paris: Flammarion, 2001.

Biehn, Michel. *Cooking with Herbs: The Flavor of Provence*. Paris: Flammarion, 2001.

Collas, Philippe and Villedary, Éric. *Edith Wharton's French Riviera*. Paris: Flammarion, 2002.

Cros, Philippe. *The Painters of Provence*. Paris: Flammarion, 2001.

Duck, Noëlle. *Provence Style*. Paris: Flammarion, 2002.

Jones, Louisa and Motte, Vincent. *Gardens in Provence*. Paris: Flammarion, 2002.

Jones, Louisa and Motte, Vincent. *Gardens of the French Riviera*. Paris: Flammarion, 2002.

OTHER TITLES

Attlee, Helena and Ramsay, Alex (photographer). *The Most Beautiful Country Towns of Provence*. London: Thames & Hudson, 2002.

Biehn, Michel. *Colors of Provence*. New York: Stewart, Tabori, & Chang, 2002.

Chamberlain, Samuel. *Domestic Architecture in Rural France*. New York: Architectural Book Publishing Company, 1981.

Jacobs, Michael and Palmer, Hugh. *The Most Beautiful Villages of Provence*. London: Thames & Hudson, 1994.

Jones, Louisa. *Provence: A Country Almanac*. New York: Stewart, Tabori, & Chang, 1999.

Krohn, Don. *In the South of France* (Imago Mundi Book). Boston: David R Godine, 1999.

Laws, Bill. *Traditional Houses of Rural France*. New York: Abbeville Press, 1997.

Lenard, Yvonne. *The Magic of Provence: Pleasures of Southern France*. New Jersey: Princeton Book Company, 2000.

Long, Dixon, et al. *Markets of Provence: A Culinary Tour of Southern France*. San Francisco: Collins, 1996.

Lovatt-Smith, Lisa ed. and Muthesius, A. ed. *Provence Interiors*. New York: Taschen America LLC, 1997.

Mayle, Peter. *A Year in Provence*. New York: Vintage, 1991.

Mayle, Peter. *Encore Provence: More Adventures in the South of France*. New York: Vintage, 2000.

More, Julian. *Tour de Provence*. Vermont: Trafalgar Square, 2001.

Onley, Richard, ed. *Provence, the Beautiful Cookbook: Authentic Recipes from the Regions of Provence*. San Francisco: Collins, 1993.

Phillips, Betty Lou and Pissack, Dan. *Provençal Interiors: French Country Style in America*. Utah: Gibbs Smith Publisher, 1998.

Toman, Rolf. *Provence-Art: Architecture and Landscape*. Cologne: Könemann, 2000.

Wells, Patricia. *At Home in Provence*. New York: Scribner, 1996.

Williams, Roger and Brown, Deni. *Provence and Côte d'Azur*. London: Dorling Kindersley Publishing, 1997.

GUIDES TO THE REGION

Coons, Nancy and Franken, Owen (photographer). *Fodor's Escape to Provence*. Fodor's Travel Publications, Fabrizio La Roca, 2000.

Hachette Routard: *Provence & the Côte d'Azur*. Cassell & Co., 2002.

Michelin Green Guide: *Provence*. Michelin Travel Publications Ltd., 2000.

FRENCH TITLES

Beaumelle, M. et al. *Les Arts décoratifs en Provence du XVIIe au XIXe siècle*. Marseilles: Éditions J. Lafitte, 1993.

Berenson, Kathryn. *Boutis de Provence*. Paris: Flammarion, 1997.

Biehn, Michel. *En jupon piqué et robe d'Indienne*. Marseilles: Éditions Jeanne Laffitte, 1987.

Biehn, Michel. *Secrets d'Arlésiennes*. Arles: Actes Sud, 1999.

Bourgeois, J.-J. *L'Âge d'or du siège paillé*. Éditions Massin, 2000.

Clébert, Jean-Claude. *Mémoire du Luberon*. Paris: Éditions Aubanel, 19??.

Duck, Noëlle. *Routes et Chemins de Provence*. Paris: Flammarion, 2000.

Dumas, Marc. *La Faïence d'Apt et de Castellet*. Édisud, 1990.

Parisis, Jean-Louis. *Les Folies de la corniche, Marseilles 1800-1990*. Marseilles: Éditions J. Lafitte, 1999.

Silvioni, Marie and Girard-Lagorce, Sylvie. *Provence Terre de soleil*. Flammarion.

Tixier, J.-M. *Le Cabanon*. Marseilles: Éditions J. Lafitte, 1994.

INDEX

ACKNOWLEDGMENTS

DANE McDOWELL wishes to express her gratitude to all those who generously opened the doors of their homes to her. She would also like to thank Vincent Bœuf and Laura Skoler for their warm welcome, and the entire Flammarion team—particularly Gisou Bavoillot and Nathalie Démoulin— for their efficiency and patience.

CHRISTIAN SARRAMON extends special thanks to Inès, Daouia Bellal and Didier Tisseyre, Pierre Bels and Ysabel de Roquette, Christine and Alain Depauw, Barbara and Jules Farber, Brigitte Forgeur, Danielle and Jean-Claude Gandon, Nello Renault, and Linda Koreska.

THE EDITORS would like to thank all those who have contributed over the years to their growing appreciation of Provence, particularly Olivier Baussan, Michel Biehn, Vincent Bœuf, Elisabeth and Philippe Bourgeois, Marguerite and Marc Dumas, Astrid and Gianni Ladu, Edith Mézard, and Patricia and Walter Wells. To the owners of all the homes and gardens appearing in the present volume, they also wish to express gratitude for the warm welcome extended to the entire production team. Thanks also to Emmanuelle Bons, Emmanuelle Devaux, Fanny Pampouille, Sylvie Ramaut, and Nathalie Zberro for their invaluable help in making this book reality.

IN THE SAME COLLECTION

Editor
Ghislaine Bavoillot

Translated from the French by
Louise Guiney

Copy-editing and typesetting
Penelope Isaac

Proofreading
Slade Smith

Art direction
Karen Bowen

Cartography
Édigraphie, Rouen

Color separation
Articrom, Milan

Originally published as
L'Art de vivre en Provence
© Flammarion 2002

English-language edition
© Flammarion 2003
ISBN: 2-0801-1139-6
FA1139-03-I
Dépôt légal: 01/2003

Photos of Le Corbusier's cabin
in Roquebrune-Cap-Martin
© FLC–Adagp, Paris.

All rights reserved. No part of this publication may be reproduced in any form or by any means, electronic, photocopy, information retrieval system, or otherwise, without written permission from Flammarion.

Printed in Italy by Canale